Pages of Passion Book 1: My First 19 Years

An Autobiography

George Hatcher

Previously published as Billion Dollar Rainmaker Part I in 2021

This book can be purchased at over 40,000 bookstores and libraries, including brick-and-mortar stores, online, in print and digital, including Apple, Kindle, and Audible formats. Casa Hatcher Press books are available at special quantity discounts for bulk purchases, sales promotions, premiums, and educational use for fundraising. Casa Hatcher Press is a subsidiary of Pretty Face, Inc., Rancho Mirage, California 92270.

For details, contact:

Casa Hatcher Press. http://casahatcherpress.com (800) 416-6189

Copyright © 2024 by George Hatcher. All rights reserved. Printed in the United States of America and abroad.

No part of this book may be used in any manner except in the case of brief quotations in critical articles or reviews.

Book and cover designed by Casa Hatcher Press

Pages of Passion Book 1: My First 19 Years by George Hatcher

First Edition 2024

LCCN: 2024905461

ISBN: 979-8-9882886-1-9 (Hardback)

ISBN: 979-8-9882886-2-6 (Paperback)

ISBN: 979-8-9882886-3-3 (Ebook-EPUB)

Introduction

True Reflections: Echoes of a Life Remembered

As you embark on this journey through my life, I want to share a crucial aspect of my storytelling. While the names of individuals, places, and establishments may have been altered to protect their identities and privacy, and while memory may sometimes falter and details may blur with time, one truth remains unwavering – the essence of the story is real.

In this tapestry of recollections, woven with threads of honesty and nostalgia, what stands firm amidst the changes and uncertainties is the authenticity of my experiences. So, as you delve into these pages and navigate the twists and turns of my narrative, remember this: no matter the alterations, no matter the imperfections in remembrance, the heart of the tale beats with the rhythm of truth.

Pictures In This Book

Dear Reader,

As you embark on this journey through my life, I want to share a unique aspect of this autobiography. Alongside my words, you will find a handful of selected images that complement my stories and memories. While these photos are not direct representations of the individuals I've written about, they serve to illustrate and evoke the essence of my experiences. For instance, my third wife is referred to as Sophia in this narrative, but it's important to note that "Sophia" is not her real name, and the AI-generated image representing her does not depict her alone; it captures the essence of a character playing the part of Sophia in my book.

In reflecting on my life, I've included images of significant people, places, and moments that shaped who I am today. From a stock photo of a child delivering canned food—reminiscent of my industrious youth when I sold canned goods I received from my father—to a vibrant portrayal of lettuce in the fields, reminding me of the days my dad took me to the lettuce fields, where workers picked lettuce and loaded his truck with crates of it, these visuals add another layer to my narrative.

Additionally, I've illustrated elements of my father's business, particularly a striking image of garlic, which represents the hard work and dedication that defined his life. These images are not just decorative; they are meant to enhance your understanding and connection to the stories I share.

Thank you for joining me on this personal journey. I hope these images enrich your reading experience and allow you to visualize my memories as vividly as I have.

Dedication

Molly,

In the dance of life, you are my steady partner,

and in every melody, you are my cherished harmony.

With enduring love,

George

Acknowledgments

I would like to express my deepest gratitude to my dedicated editor, Allie. Your unwavering support and expertise have been invaluable throughout the years. I sincerely hope for your swift recovery and eagerly anticipate your return to delve into my new literary works.

A special thank you to J.B. for your tremendous assistance in preparing my books for publication and for your brilliant ideas that brought the book covers to life. Your contribution has truly enhanced the essence of my work.

Thank you to both Allie and J.B. for your exceptional dedication and creativity that have helped bring my words to fruition.

WARNING!

Adult matter

This book is designed for an adult audience. It contains themes of violence and sexual behavior that are not suitable for minors, sensitive readers, or individuals living in the current chaotic world, where incurable sexually transmitted diseases and a pandemic have confined us to solitary spaces within our homes. While my life is not a work of fiction, the names of some individuals I have encountered have been altered to preserve their privacy.

All of the characters, organizations, and events depicted in this novel have likely been shaped by the passage of time, forgetfulness, and a timeline that was adjusted for the sake of expediency.

Also by George Hatcher

Mario 1: Woman in Jeopardy

Mario 2: Coming Of Age

Mario 3: Risky Business

Mario 4: Free Fall

Mario 5: Afire

Mario 6: Marked

Mario 7: Aftershock

Mario 8: Captivated

One Wilshire

Pretty Face

Arabe

Gabi

Rico

Cats: Meow is the Language of Love

Billion Dollar Rainmaker Part I

Pages of Passion Book 1: My First 19 Years

Coming Soon

Pages of Passion Book 2: Bold Beginnings

Mario 9

Rico Santos, Part 2

Gabi 2

Contents

1. The Immigrant's Legacy — 1
2. Los Angeles - Bright Lights Big City — 27
3. Getting Sorted Out — 36
4. Hollenbeck Junior High — 52
5. A New Job — 74
6. Twists of Fate — 92
7. About Selena — 103
8. I joined the Navy — 135
9. Selena Returns — 144
10. The Promise of Forever — 149
11. Juarez, Mexico — 152
12. Fast Friends — 169
13. El Keno — 174
14. The Feds — 185
15. Pancho's Body Shop — 194
16. Hangovers Are Not Fun — 200
17. Selena's Shopping — 205
18. Selena's Secret — 209
19. The End Of Us — 224
20. Selena Was Truly Gone — 228
21. The Bravest Woman I Would Ever Know — 232
22. Train Ride — 238
23. Such a Fool — 249
24. Marine Brig — 257
25. Freedom Delayed — 266
26. New Chances, Old Patter — 280

About the Author — 287

Chapter 1
The Immigrant's Legacy

When I was born on October 9th, 1942, my sixty-year-old father named me George Azar Kuri, Jr, but I believe my story really begins when my father came to America. At fourteen, sure that he could share in the American pot of gold, my dad left behind his mother and nine brothers and sisters. On her knees out in the street in front of where they lived in Beirut, my grandmother pleaded for him not to go, but go he did, stowaway on a merchant ship.

After a month in the US, he made his way to Detroit, Michigan. Although he was fluent in three languages, English wasn't one of them, so it was a rough start. He bought a shoe-shine box and tools of the trade and found refuge with other kids hustling the streets. He began learning English.

The other kids teased him for spending his first dollars on new trousers, a shirt, and shoes, but new clothes got him permission to shine shoes in front of the Cadillac Hotel. During his second month there, he shined the shoes of John Apple, a big, blustery man from Arizona.

I imagine this conversation.

"Where you from, George? I notice you have an accent."

"I'm from Syria, sir. Where are you from?"

By the third morning, the conversation lasted longer than the shine.

"What language do they speak in Syria, boy?"

"Arabic, sir. But I speak French, too, and one day I will speak English good."

"Come to Arizona with me, and you can be my houseboy. You teach me French and be loyal to me, and you'll never lack anything."

My dad agreed.

John Apple was a friendly man, an opportunist. Or maybe he just felt compassion for a fourteen-year-old alone in a foreign country. The rumor was that Mr. Apple and his friend, Mr. Douglas, owned and ran Douglas, Arizona, and the neighboring town of Agua Prieta, Mexico. There were only two mansions around, each occupying one of them.

As my father grew, so did Mr. Apple's appreciation. Apple sat him down for a serious talk when he'd been there a year.

"George, your aptitude for English, Spanish, and numbers is amazing," he said. "I need your smarts at my warehouse."

My dad had no choice. He told me once that he had to learn Spanish because Apple was fluent in Spanish. Everyone who worked at Apple's house was from Agua Prieta and only spoke Spanish.

My father, with his language skills and his knack for math, went to work as assistant manager of the only wholesale grocery warehouse in a hundred square miles. Two years later, at seventeen, he opened his own distribution warehouse on the Mexican side of the border. My dad's distribution house stocked all American products, canned foods, dairy, candy, gum, janitorial supplies, pots & pans, flatware, and paper products like cups, napkins, etc. My dad's Agua Prieta customers were shopping at his warehouse to avoid crossing the border to Douglas to buy from Apple's warehouse. Apple was smart. As my dad's partner, he held fifty percent ownership of the Mexican store. I'd say that offset his loss of business. The warehouse had pretty much everything store owners wanted to resell to people in Agua Prieta. If someone who wasn't a store owner came in, they had to pay the retail price.

It was the turn of the century.

My father became rich like his benefactors, Mr. Apple and Mr. Douglas. It always sounded like a fairytale that my dad got rich so fast. Then again, what is wealthy to a seventeen-year-old immigrant who grew up in impoverished circumstances in Beirut? I don't know the timeline or what it took to be what he called rich. Anything is possible. If my dad became rich, then Apple became richer.

When I came on the scene, my father had been in that border town for fifty years. He had been married and widowed four times and fathered twelve children, three sons and nine daughters, from previous marriages. My mother gave birth to my brother Raul eight years before I was born. I never learned if my mom already had Raul when she married my dad or if Raul is my half-brother. I know that my brother is eight years older than me, and his birthdate is the same as mine: October 9th. My mom was secretive, or maybe I wasn't inquisitive.

My mother, petite and barely five feet tall, possessed the striking black hair and eyes characteristic of her Mexican heritage. In contrast, my father, standing at six feet four inches, was slim and distinguished-looking, with fair skin and light eyes. Their differences were unmistakable. However, it's noteworthy that my maternal grandparents were from Spain and had immigrated to Mexico, which explains my mother's Latin looks and fair complexion, resembling her Spanish roots. As for me, I grew to medium height, inherited my mother's Latin features, and acquired my father's hazel eyes. After several visits to Beirut, I came to realize that my appearance and coloring align closely with that of an individual from that region.

My father was a solitary man and tough, the last of the

pioneers. He had his unique style and wore a forties-style hat and overcoat until the end of his days.

I wasn't born into a mansion. By the time I was born in 1942, my father was not at his financial apex. He still had his hand in several businesses that gave him sufficient income to keep his status with the Douglas pioneers. He was a high-ranking member of the Elks Club, the Lions Club, the Chamber of Commerce, and the Knights of Columbus.

I basically grew up in the back rooms of my folks' curio and flower shop in Agua Prieta, Mexico. Yep, I was actually born in one of those rooms and stayed put until we made the move to a home in Douglas, Arizona, just a skip across the border. And let me tell you, while my parents were hustling at the store where we lived, I had a Nanny taking care of me and making sure I was safe and having fun.

I remember a collie named Thunder who was tragically killed by a truck that carelessly veered over the curb while the driver was attempting to park in front of a nearby hardware store. It was a sunny day, and I was out for a leisurely walk with Nanny and Thunder, enjoying the fresh air and the company of our beloved pet. Suddenly, the peaceful atmosphere was shattered as the truck unexpectedly crashed into the wall of the store, causing a loud and jarring impact.

In that split second, Thunder instinctively sprang into action, pushing Nanny and me out of harm's way with incredible strength and bravery. It was a selfless act of protection that I will never forget. However, Thunder's heroic efforts came at a great cost. The force of the collision was too much for our loyal companion to bear, and he tragically lost his life in the process.

Even though I was just a young child of three at the time, the memory of that heartbreaking event remains vivid in my mind. I can still recall the overwhelming sense of sadness and loss that washed over me as I realized that Thunder was gone forever. It is a testament to the profound impact that our furry friends can have on our lives, even at such a tender age.

Agua Prieta was a tourist town kept alive by American dollars. Across the border, Douglas had sprung up from an old cattle town around the Copper Queen smelter, a mine in the Arizona desert. Around half of its inhabitants worked the mine and owed their souls to the company store. The other half were supplied provisions by John Apple. Somewhere along the line, my dad was no longer in the same business as John Apple, perhaps why he was no longer wealthy.

Douglas was a clean and prosperous small American town with broad streets and sidewalks, a JCPenney, a Newberry's, a Sears, and a hospital. Agua Prieta was a typical Mexican border town, colorful and wild, catering to the kinkiest whims of American guests, its lifeblood.

My mom was just as hardworking as my dad. During one of my dad's slower periods when the curio store wasn't bringing in much business, she decided to work at one of the two flower shops in Douglas and learned the ins and outs of the business. People would often go to Douglas for flowers until she opened the only flower shop on the Mexican side of the border in Aqua Prieta. The curio shop space was divided in half, and my mom set up the flower shop there. As a result, my childhood was filled with constant employment as a ring-bearer at weddings. It felt like I was always surrounded by flowers. I've probably attended more weddings than most people who aren't ordained in the clergy. Perhaps that's what made me feel so comfortable and natural when it came to the idea of being a husband myself.

I often asked my mom, "Why me, don't they have children?"

My mom always had the same answer, "Your curly hair and beautiful eyes." Followed by a kiss.

My mother's shop was next to a nudie bar, which offered a Mexican delicacy, turtle meat cocktails. Some of my earliest memories are of playing outside the flower shop and riding on the backs of the huge turtles kept as livestock by the bar's owners. I would ride turtle-back, imagining myself sitting on a horse, bull, or even an elephant. Then my mother's voice would break the reverie.

"¡Georgie! ¡Ven a lavarte y vestirte para la boda!"

"Georgie! Come get washed and dressed for the wedding!" My mom only spoke Spanish.

During my first few years, my father was in one of the down cycles of his up-and-down existence. He might one day be scraping, and the next be rich again, but few people could learn which day it was by talking to him. He always behaved as if it were still those early years when he was rich before my mother was even born. My mother always told me that my dad was not as rich as his stories. She bad-mouthed my dad as far back as I can remember, but it didn't matter to me. I loved them both, so I ignored the friction between them, just as I ignored his yelling that she was a flirtatious woman who didn't respect their marriage. Clearly, my dad was jealous. As far as I know, he never touched my mom in anger, but they screamed at each other a lot, my dad in English, my mother in Spanish.

At the age of five, we transitioned from the back rooms of the stores to the newly constructed cinderblock home in Douglas. In those days, acquiring a house in Douglas meant purchasing an empty lot and constructing the house.

"I love you, my son," Dad said, hugging me when we moved in. It made me feel terrific when he said, "My favorite son, I built this home just for you. It's your home."

"I adore my home, Papa! I love having my very own room!"

I adored that house, with its roof and everything. My father assured me that no tornado or hurricane could harm our home. "The roof," he said, "could never burn." It had a copper-colored asbestos shingle. It's ironic - I now laugh at that. He was proud of that roof. I don't think Douglas ever experienced a tornado or a hurricane. I'm not sure if it's important whether my mother kept lilies in the living room, and although I can vividly picture it from my seventy-year-old memory, I wish I had a photograph of the house. It wasn't large.

It wasn't small either. It was on a big lot. In Douglas, the big houses, the so-called mansions, had porches. Ours had a big porch. Before you hit the entry, you had to go up three stairs to get to the door to get in. We had lathe and plaster walls, eight-foot-high ceilings, a living room, dining room, kitchen, pantry, and three bedrooms. In the back, we had another porch, but it was enclosed. It was so big my mother kept the washing machine out there—a Bendix. I remember.

My mom and dad had a bedroom, my brother had his, and I had mine. It was a plain house with two bathrooms and nice, highly polished hardwood floors. Looking back to when I was five, six, and seven, I can't describe the furniture except that it was nice.

When you entered the backyard, there were fruit trees. My mother and father had a great love for plants, and they planted grapevines. Perhaps it's a tradition from Syria— my father planted fruit trees and would dig water ditches all around them. We had around thirty trees.

My father had a carpenter construct a playhouse hidden behind the trees, which became my personal chemistry lab. Especially after receiving a chemistry set for Christmas. I delved into experiments with phosphorus and various other substances within that space. Adjacent to the playhouse, there stood a substantial cage that I eventually filled with pigeons of diverse breeds. My fondness for birds was evident, as I frequently left the cage open. Yet despite lacking formal knowledge or training, the birds never strayed. Coincidentally, my mother also possessed a large birdcage, the origins of which I'm uncertain about, but it housed a multitude of canaries. Our affinity for birds seems to have deep roots within our family history.

We lived on ninth street, an area that boasted truly magnificent residences. It's important to note that the truly grand houses belonged to the Copper Queen Smelter, providing accommodations for their executives in town. Our neighbors, who were doctors, also resided in lovely houses, although not as grand as those owned by the Copper Queen Smelter executives. This distinction set the tone for the neighborhood.

Our neighbors were incredibly friendly. I have fond memories of one particular neighbor who lived across the street. She would often step out with a tray in hand and call out, "You-Who, come get these goodies I just baked." Another neighbor would come over to offer me a refreshing glass of lemonade while I played in the front yard. Their acts of kindness and warmth added to the sense of community that we cherished.

The frequent arguments between my parents left a deep impression on me, particularly during the times when they went to visit Ron Simon, a relative of my father's. My dad had played a pivotal role in bringing Simon to the United States, and Simon had evolved into a prosperous business owner with multiple grocery stores, a nightclub in Agua Prieta, and a bar with numerous pool tables.

During these visits to his opulent home, I was always given the privilege of sitting in his Cadillac. It was only later that I discovered the true purpose of these visits, as my parents sought counsel from Simon in an effort to resolve their ongoing conflicts. Understanding this context helped me comprehend why my mom would sit right next to my dad in the car on the way home from Simon's and exchange kisses, making me feel reassured. This memory remains vivid in my mind.

From my earliest days, my dad had pointed out the big mansion that had been his next to those of Mr. Douglas and Mr. Apple. Looking back with adult eyes, I can see that the houses were just big homes, not what I would now call mansions. Over the years, as I grew up, many homes were built in the area for the Copper Queen Smelter executives, homes I frequently visited because I went to school with the children of the big shots. The home dad had built for us was much smaller - one story - but I loved it. It was mine. I no longer looked enviously at the home that had been his.

At the age of five, as I began attending school, I was a cheerful boy who had never encountered a moment of distress. However, my lack of proficiency in English became a considerable setback. While everyone in my class was fluent in English, I struggled to overcome this mental barrier. Learning English pronunciation proved to be particularly challenging, to the extent that even now, many decades later, I vividly recall the difficulties I faced.

One memory that stands out is that of Sister Ann at school, who often exhibited frustration due to my struggles. During one such incident, she confronted me, and I could feel her agitated breath on my face as she urged me: "For the last time, George, say the word 'blackboard.'" I can still recall the discomfort I felt as the peach-fuzz on the back of my neck bristled. The other children's laughter only added to my embarrassment. "Blockboad," I nervously uttered, my voice trembling as I fought back a childish giggle. This experience left me feeling anxious and exceedingly self-conscious.

Sister Ann must have perceived my attempt as a jest, and in response, she slapped me. The sound of her slap pierced the air before the sting registered. Overwhelmed with shame and embarrassment, I reacted instinctively and abruptly fled the classroom, sprinting away from Sister Ann and the jeering children at their desks. I ran the seven blocks back to my house, consumed by tears and distress. I pleaded with my father and mother, declaring that I could never return to that school.

As a result, I never set foot in Catholic school again and instead enrolled in public school. By the end of the first grade, I had made considerable progress with my English. Once I had a firm grasp of the language, school became an enjoyable experience. Things fell into place more effortlessly, and my teacher praised my intellect and strong memory. However, it took a considerable amount of time before I shed my accent.

After I started learning English pretty well in school, my father and I communicated in English, while my mother and I continued to converse in Spanish. In an effort to enhance her English-speaking skills, my mother started attending evening classes taught by a dedicated teacher who came to our home. Despite her determination to be able to communicate with me in English, she faced the same struggle I did – a block that seemed insurmountable. It would take many years before my mother finally mastered the art of writing and speaking English, eventually even graduating from high school.

My parents were proud of me but argued about my future. Life with my father had not proved to be entirely secure. My mother had been a nurse when she met my dad and wanted me to be a professional man. But my father had the passions of an entrepreneur.

"He's going to be a doctor," my mom shouted. "Not a merchant like you."

"Nothing wrong with being a merchant. He can be rich as I once was."

"Don't poison his mind."

My mom was something else.

* * *

I spent a significant amount of time with my parents at their business on the Mexico side of the border in Agua Prieta. My father, who had left Syria for the United States at the tender age of 14, imparted to me a wealth of knowledge about cutlery. Even though I wonder if he ever had the opportunity to attend school, his remarkable intellect and proficiency in multiple languages never ceased to amaze me. His expertise in cutlery was truly impressive, considering he had once owned a curio gift store filled with sterling silver from Taxco. The display cases were brimming with a diverse array of sterling silver items, all available for sale.

Under my father's tutelage, I learned about the intricate details of forks, knives, spoons, and even serving utensils. While I couldn't discern the true value of the sterling silver he sold, he patiently taught my brother and me proper table manners using the cutlery, explaining which fork to use with steak, the appropriate fork for salad, and so on. He even instructed us on the art of carving meat using a knife and fork, as well as the finer points of setting a table including the placement of a bread plate and butter knife. My curiosity led me to inquire about large plates that we never used, and in response, my father introduced me to the concept of charger plates and how they were traditionally used in a formal setting.

I once asked my father why we didn't use such fine flatware at home and why he stocked such elegant items at the store. There was a thoughtful pause before he responded, "That's a great question for your mother." This insight into my father's remarkable knowledge and abilities continues to astound me, and I often find myself pondering how he acquired such meticulous expertise, wondering if it stemmed from his role as a purveyor of these wares to discerning customers.

* * *

When I was at the tender age of eight, my father experienced one of his periods of financial struggle. In order to maintain the mortgage payments, he made the difficult decision to rent out our home, along with all our furniture, to an executive from the mining company. He remained unwavering in his belief that we would reclaim our residence one day.

As a result, we relocated to a modest furnished apartment. Each afternoon, after school, I would pass by our former beautiful home and silently yearn for the day we would return. I made every effort to be brave in the face of losing our house, but my disappointment manifested in the declining grades on my report cards. The straight-A student I once was now found himself struggling with C's. Perhaps I was subconsciously searching for an excuse to justify my waning interest in certain subjects.

My time in that apartment was filled with misery, and Christmas Eve proved to be the most challenging. Beneath the meager tree, I found my present—a simple bar of candy. It was on that day that I came to the crushing realization that there was no Santa Claus. Despite my disillusionment, I endeavored to shield my parents from the hurt. "Thanks, Papa. I love Snickers," I uttered, masking my disappointment.

With a sense of optimism, my mother reassured me, "Next year will be better." I kissed her and responded, "I know, Mama. I don't mind being poor. Honest," even though it was a lie.

My dad bought canned goods from a packing plant in Agua Prieta and sold them to stores. Mostly small markets across the border in Douglas where we lived. At times when things weren't going well, he also sold lots of other things. That's when I decided to take the initiative.

I would load up my four-wheel wagon and pull it along the sidewalk. At each house, I rang the bell and asked our neighbors if they wanted to buy a can of shredded beef. I would explain that all they needed to do was heat it up or fry it and add onions and tomatoes, just like my mother did. I can't remember if I sold them for a quarter a can, but I do remember that I'd sell out.

After the first time, I pestered my dad to bring more home because the neighbors were waving me down when I passed their houses, wanting to buy the great treat that I had introduced them to.

My dad once brought me along with a crew of men he hired to harvest lettuce not far from home. The men took great care in cutting the lettuce so it would grow again. I remember the scent of the cut lettuce, the fragrant field dirt, the perfectly aligned rows, and especially when my dad caught me kicking the lettuce like they were fluffy green footballs. My dad put a stop to that as soon as he saw me doing it. "That is disgraceful!" he scolded me. He never spanked me.

Filled to the brim with crates of lettuce, the big truck came home with us. In the morning, my dad drove the truck and me to Los Angeles. We arrived in the evening and spent the night at an old hotel on 7th and Central in the heart of the old wholesale produce market. At the crack of dawn, we were in the market, and before an hour passed, my father sold the lettuce to an outlet. At eight, I couldn't have understood how my father hustled, but I see and appreciate it now. I waited in the truck while the crates were unloaded. Right after breakfast, we were on the road back to Douglas. I slept a long time while my dad drove and sang in Arabic. I suppose that was my first time in Los Angeles.

My father took me around to garlic farms close to Agua Prieta where he was greeted warmly, and sometimes we had lunch with the owners. My dad would give the owner cash. Not for the meal, but to help the farmer with expenses. Eight months later when the garlic was harvested, the farmer would sell the harvest to my father who in turn sold it to distributors.

Further away from our home, there were farmers who cultivated chiltepin peppers, which were small, round, and incredibly spicy. My dad would provide these farmers with financial assistance, and later return to purchase their harvest in order to sell them in markets like Los Angeles.

The peppers resembled peas in shape, but unlike peas, they were vibrant red in color. I can still recall the intense aroma of the fiery chilis, as well as the sight of a truck filled to the brim with large burlap sacks overflowing with these little round red peppers.

* * *

In the late forties and early fifties, my dad found various entrepreneurial opportunities to meet the demand for specific products. One such endeavor involved store scales, particularly those produced by Toledo, designed to weigh and display in pounds. Recognizing the local need for scales calibrated in kilos, he undertook the task of converting these scales to match the regional measurement standards. Following the successful modifications, he then supplied these customized scales to markets in Agua Prieta and neighboring towns.

Additionally, my father extended his expertise to cash registers, recognizing the necessity to adapt these machines to display pesos instead of dollars. His technical acumen and commitment to meeting local demands were evident as he diligently worked to modify the cash registers, ensuring they were tailored to the currency needs of the community.

Moreover, my father also identified an opportunity within the butcher shops of Mexico. Understanding the preference for US-made electric meat saws, he ventured into purchasing these sought-after saws in the United States and introduced them to the butcher shops in Agua

Prieta and nearby areas. This initiative further demonstrated his entrepreneurial intuition and commitment to addressing the specific needs of local businesses.

Reflecting on my father's myriad endeavors, it is evident that his efforts were driven by a deep understanding of the local market and a steadfast commitment to offering customized solutions to businesses in the region. Despite his remarkable contributions, it is important to note that these undertakings did not lead to substantial wealth or affluence for my father. Nonetheless, his industrious nature and impactful initiatives resonate as a testament to his resilient spirit and dedication to serving the community.

When I was nine, things began to look better. My dad bought a brand-new car. We moved back home. In my prayers, I thanked God for giving me back my house. Every day, I would count the cash stuffed into one of my dad's dresser drawers. My mom had evening gloves for the gala balls in Agua Prieta. In my mother's dresser, where she kept those long evening gloves, I found neatly rolled hundred-dollar bills stuffed into the gloves' fingers. This money was from my dad's import and export business, not my mother's flower shop. It reassured me to look at the money each day. I was convinced that as long as there was money in these places, we would never have to move again. I brought home A's again. Today, I can't say that the house was entirely responsible for my bouncing back to better grades.

My dad let me have a paper route. I saved most of my money in the event there might be a future crisis that might mean having to move again. After putting a rubber band around each edition, I wrapped the newspapers, then I packed them into canvas bags, one on each side of the handlebars. At first, I had to get used to the weight. When I got good, I avoided returning for more papers by packing another bag on the back of the bike. It took a while to remember what houses got a paper. At first, it drove me crazy to be looking at the subscribers' addresses in the small notepad the newspaper manager had given me.

My childhood was anything but ordinary. At the young age of seven, I eagerly joined the Cub Scouts and looked forward to their weekly meetings. Beyond scouting, I had a tight-knit group of friends with whom I spent my after-school hours. We relished activities like playing pool at a friend's house and exploring the nearby desert on mule rides. Despite the urbanization of most of Douglas, the desert with its captivating cacti and diverse creatures was just a stone's throw away. Looking back, it's amusing to realize that I had at least two girlfriends by the tender age of nine. I had a passion for roller skating and biking, and I distinctly remember bringing a mule home from the desert and pretending to ride it like a horse, just as any nine-year-old would do.

My mother had her reservations, especially when I brought home not one, but two donkeys. "You want to have a donkey here, you need to clean up after him," she would say. Her concern grew when a second donkey made an appearance, prompting her to exclaim, "You can have one, not two!" As if that wasn't enough, when the donkeys started nibbling at the fruit trees, my mom and dad put their foot down, declaring, "No more donkeys on the property."

Reflecting on my childhood, I vividly recall the immense sense of pride I felt when I made the transition from the Cub Scouts to the Boy Scouts around the age of nine. With the earnings from my newspaper job, I purchased my own Boy Scouts uniform and all the necessary gear. The first time I wore it, I was filled with a deep sense of accomplishment and pride, which was shared by my friends. It was a defining moment that underscored the significance of the uniform and the strong sense of belonging it brought to us.

* * *

At nine, I was slim and healthy with curly hair. One of my friends had a thirteen-year-old sister named Valita. One day she caught me staring at her, and she asked me why. I told her the truth. It was because I thought she was beautiful. A couple days later, when I was at her house on an overnight in a backyard tent with her brother, when her brother was in the house for something, she poked her head in the tent, smiled, and told me to follow her. I followed her to the garage, where her parents had two cars. In the farthest darkest corner, she put her arms around me and told me to tell her again that she was beautiful. We could barely see in the dark.

"You're beautiful, Valita," I said.

Then she kissed me. It was my first kiss.

"Give me your hand. Are you curious?" Valita asked.

I couldn't see that well, but I knew her shorts were around her ankles. After she put my hand there so I could touch her, she laughed softly. I saw her pull her shorts up, and we walked out.

"One day, we need to play doctor, Georgie," she said.

To this day, I remember the scent of her. It's fascinating to me how certain scents can have such a strong impact on our memories. I was nine years old!

I was aware that my actions were wrong. The following morning, I visited the Catholic Church we regularly attended. Fortunately, the premises were empty. I knelt down and made my way to the altar, fervently seeking forgiveness from God. However, I chose not to disclose this transgression during confession with the priest. I simply couldn't bring myself to do so. This incident never recurred, and yet, Valita always greeted me with a smile whenever our paths crossed. Her brother remained oblivious. This was perhaps my earliest significant secret.

By the way, I took catechism classes for months as a child and received confirmation and holy communion. I was baptized as a newborn but don't remember.

When I was ten years old, my mom told me we were moving to Los Angeles. She was divorcing my dad. They sold my beautiful house and my mom received one thousand dollars[1] that she put in an account at the Bank of Douglas. I was with her. She was given a checkbook. My older brother had already left for Mexico City to study at the University of Mexico. I was heartbroken, although now I'm not sure what upset me the most, having to leave my dad or leaving my beautiful house again.

Decades later, when I was consulting with a law firm in Los Angeles, developing a case against the Copper Queen giant that owned a smelter in Douglas and mined for copper in Bisbee, Arizona, I drove by the house that I had been so fond of. It is tiny in comparison to where I live now in California. It was not beautiful at all. It was badly in need of love and care. Things look bigger than they are when you're a kid.

---

1. $1,000 in 1952 equates to about $10,000 in 2020

Chapter 2
Los Angeles - Bright Lights Big City

My mom and I took a Greyhound bus to Los Angeles. Why Los Angeles? I don't know. Maybe because I had a stepbrother named Sam there who had six children. We had visited him once, and my mom took a liking to the big city. Big cities didn't frighten my mom. Probably because she had lived in Mexico City for many years.

My mom explained we would not be seeing my dad's son or my cousins because of the divorce. The bottom line is that we knew no one in Los Angeles apart from my stepbrother Sam, whom we were not going to meet up with.

It was early morning when the driver announced that we were minutes from the Greyhound depot. The bus was moving too fast. I was in no hurry to arrive in a strange city. I had left behind all my friends and everything familiar. I looked out the window at the fog, which I had never seen before, and huge palm trees like those I had only seen in movies.

"We're here," my mother said in Spanish. "Our new home."

My mom had to be scared. Why didn't she show it? She was smiling.

We stood outside the depot on the dirty corner of Sixth & Los Angeles. The fog had lifted enough that I saw bums milling around. There were no people like that in Douglas.

"Do you have your checkbook and money, Mama?" I asked.

"Yes," she replied, "and I have a little over two hundred in cash."

"Good," I said.

"Don't be scared, son. I'm with you."

"Mamá, no tengo miedo," I replied.

"Since she couldn't speak English, it was up to me to navigate our way around. Despite the English classes she took in Douglas, it seemed as though she had learned nothing. I pushed aside my apprehension and said, "Mama, lets walk. We'll find a hotel to stay in until we figure out our next steps."

"Good idea," she replied.

We had a folding cart that I thought was nifty. If I stacked the suitcases just right, I could get four of them on the two-wheeled baggage cart. It was heavy for me, but I was not fragile. I managed okay, and my mom had her own strength. She carried the other two suitcases with her purse around her shoulder. I see the picture of us as I write this. Everything we owned was in that luggage.

The sign outside the Hotel Chandler at Eighth and Main read: "CLEAN ROOMS WITH KITCHEN $15.00 WEEK."

We peered through the large plate glass window and observed a group of elderly individuals gathered around a television set. Prior to this moment, the only television I had ever encountered was at the Douglas Elks Club, a place my father frequently took my mother and me for meals. Although not as extravagant as the Gadsden Hotel in Douglas, my mother assured me that it appeared clean, and the weekly cost of fifteen dollars seemed reasonable. This perception was influenced by the fact that my mother possessed a thousand dollars in the bank and two hundred dollars in cash. However, in hindsight, the fifteen dollars per week was not a favorable deal. Particularly considering our limited financial resources.

"Are you sure, Mom?" I guess it helped that until we left Douglas, I was always active and social, and not just in the Cub Scouts. I had encounters with my customers to whom I delivered newspapers and the neighbors to whom I sold canned food, not to mention the trips I took with my dad to places where he bought and sold goods. I was a kid, but I interacted with everyone. I was not shy. I was not easily scared.

"I'm sure, dear." my mom said. "Let's go inside."

The lobby was carpeted in faded red wool, threadbare in spots. It smelled like dust and perfume. Perched on a stool, a thin older man presided over the desk. I tried to bargain with him for a lower rate, but this wasn't Mexico. He wouldn't budge. "What if we pay for two weeks in advance," I offered. The clerk smiled. My mom didn't understand.

"Sorry, son, the price is fifteen dollars."

The room was small, with a tiny kitchenette, a full-sized bed, and a sagging mattress. After my mother had cleaned it, it was clean by the end of the day.

"Now what?" I asked.

"I must find a job," my mother said.

My mom was probably close to forty then. I've never been sure of her age, and she has never revealed it.

"Can we eat something first?"

I saw that wonderful smile of hers.

"We'll do better than that. We'll go eat something good, then we'll go to the show we passed on our way, and then we'll find a grocery store."

We spent hours and then days trying to find my mom a job in her former profession as a nurse. I read through the classified ads and translated each ad that was close. Even if she had gotten lucky and found a nursing job, she wouldn't have been able to pass the state test in English. She prayed for a miracle. Daily, I spent hours on the hotel lobby payphone calling jobs from the classifieds. I would explain the situation, but each time, I was turned down. They wouldn't interview her if she couldn't speak or read English. I spent hours trying to teach her.

One morning, she changed tactics and said, "Look in the paper for ads for seamstresses. I can get a job sewing."

I argued, "Mom, not that kind of work. I won't let you!"

It was funny to her that I felt that way about her working in a sewing factory. Except I knew that she had been like a doctor working for the federal health department in Mexico, traveling to troubled areas. Epidemics started from crops being irrigated with gray water instead of good water. She came in with a team backed up by soldiers that would burn the infected crops. She educated the landowners on healthy practices. However, in the US, her lack of English kept her from managing the licensing requirements of nursing. It hurt me to see her go from being a respected health worker to a poorly paid seamstress. There were too many obstacles. It had been too long since she'd been a nurse, so being a nurse in Los Angeles was never going to happen. Her English was terrible. Like me, when I started learning the language, she seemed to have a block. When my dad died, he spoke French, Arabic, Spanish, and Italian and understood German and several other languages. He was gifted like that, and he knew it. I wasn't as gifted with languages.

At some point in her life, probably during one of my dad's downturns, my mother worked in a sewing factory in Douglas. She had always had her own sewing machine, liked to sew, and could sew anything. She made curtains for the new house when we moved into it and even made them for the ugly apartment when my dad rented out the house.

The next day, I wrote down addresses for three factories. We took the bus to the first place. Ten minutes after she demonstrated that she could work a sewing machine, mom was hired for a dollar an hour. That was the going rate, so it wasn't like they were taking advantage of her. I went back to the hotel and would come back to pick her up until she got the hang of the bus stops.

I spent a lot of time watching TV with the guests in the lobby until it was time to take the bus to pick up my mom. I liked the friends I made. They were all elderly and behaved like doting grandparents, flattering and spoiling me.

One afternoon I met a tall, nicely dressed man in the lobby. He attracted my attention because he looked like a much younger version of my father. His name was Leonard Hatcher.

"Mind if I call you Leonard?" I asked.

He chuckled. "Can I call you George?"

Soon, I knew all about him. He was an elevator repairman in a garment district building. He liked the Chandler Hotel because it was clean and convenient for his work, which was two blocks away.

"You got to meet my mother. You'll like her."

"I'd like to," he said.

I had already told him about the divorce and our move alone to the big city.

"Ever think of getting married?" I asked the tall man.

Leonard had the kind of chuckle that made me want to laugh along.

"First time for everything," he said.

He treated me to a hamburger at a stand down the street.

"Did you take a day off today?"

"Matter of fact, I did."

"Are you free tonight? Do you really want to meet my mama?"

"I'd be delighted."

By the time I had to take the bus to fetch my mom, I knew even more about Leonard. He was from Oklahoma and the nicest person ever. He was a happy kind of guy and had a dozen suits. He always wore a suit and tie to his job, then changed to khakis to work, then back to the suit to come home. He learned quite a bit about me, my mother, and the house I had lost. When I left, I asked him to be in the lobby later that night so that he could meet my mother.

I told my mom, "You'll really like this man. His name is Leonard Hatcher."

I was right. A month later, they were married. My mother looked happy. Even her smile was different. Her happiness made me happy, too. Even as a kid, I knew Leonard was a good man. If he hadn't been, I don't think my mom would have taken to him.

"We'll need to move from here," Leonard said during dinner on the night they were married.

"I'll look at the ads and find something for us," I offered. "That way, you and Mama can go see what I find after you both get off of work."

"How will you get around the city?" Leonard asked.

"On the bus, of course."

I was an avid reader of the Los Angeles Times Classified Section. That's where I had found a job for my mom when we first arrived, and now, that's where I planned to find a house or apartment. I looked at all sorts of places, but the apartment Leonard finally rented was a one-bedroom across the street from Hollenbeck Park on St. Louis Street in East Los Angeles, in the heart of what we didn't know was a tough Boyle Heights barrio. The plan was for me to sleep in the dining room on a rollaway bed and stash the bed in a closet during the day.

The apartment's furniture was dingy, but we put sheets on the couch. My mother brought home fabric remnants, which she pieced together into bedspreads and furniture covers. I stopped dwelling on the house in Douglas and believed I was finally growing up.

Chapter 3
Getting Sorted Out

The first fall of my first school year in Los Angeles when I came out of the school building into the yard of Breed Street Elementary School, I discovered the four-unit building we had moved into was in one of the toughest neighborhoods in East Los Angeles.

"Hey, you! I'm talking to you."

I recognized a face I had seen in class.

"You mean me?"

"Yeah," the dark, husky kid said. He looked mean in class and even meaner face-to-face.

"You gringo or Chicano?" he asked, then turned his back to me to scribble in black crayon on the wall.

"Why'd you ask?"

I didn't like the way he turned to face me. I could see the chip on his shoulder, and I wasn't even close to trying to start anything.

"You getting smart or something, man?"

"Smart?" I tried to look surprised, but I was getting scared.

"Hey man, what's it going to be? Are you gringo or Chicano? You ain't got a Chicano name, but you look it."

"I'm Mexican and Syrian," I said, trying to figure a way to leave.

"Syrian. What's that?"

I thought a moment. "I don't know. Somewhere across the ocean somewhere. I got to go, okay?"

"I ain't finished yet. If you're Chicano, at least half, you might get in my gang. You got to be in a gang around here, man, or you're dead."

Gang? Dead? I did not know what this guy was talking about, but he sounded serious.

"You're kidding, right? I mean, dead like dead?"

"You are a wise guy, I knew it."

"You and me, we don't have anything to talk about," I said. "I don't have time for this."

He laughed. "You ain't got time to be dead, neither, huh?"

Nothing was funny, but I laughed too.

"No time. I have to find a job."

"Hey, man. I ain't said nothing funny. Why are you laughing?"

He left the wall and came closer. I quit laughing. Two of his gang buddies appeared out of nowhere. One had a frightening, disturbing giggle.

"Hey, Pi, this guy is new."

"Yeah," Pi said, standing close to me now.

"Hey," I said. "I'm new. How about we make friends? My name is George. I'm ten going on eleven soon, but I don't have any practice fighting."

That got everyone laughing.

I stretched my hand out to Pi, who was also laughing at what I said.

"Why you want to shake hands?" Pi asked. "We ain't friends."

I put my hand down. "Okay. We ain't friends."

"Hey Pi, this guy is one of them wise guys. Think we should do him in?"

The three of them surrounded me.

Pi backed off slightly.

"Later," he said. "I got to do homework tonight, or I'll catch hell tomorrow."

His friends laughed at him.

"Sissy!" one of them taunted.

Pi faced him, snarling. "Say it again, and I'll kill ya, punk."

"Kidding, Pi," the kid said.

"Hey, Pi. I don't live but a few blocks from here," I said. "If you ever need help with homework, maybe I can help."

Pi stared at me.

"Where ya live?"

"St. Louis Street. Across from the park."

"Hey, so do I." He hesitated. "You smart enough to help me with this fuckin' math?"

I smiled. "Yeah. Come on over."

Pi exchanged looks with his comrades, shrugged, and stretched out his hand.

In Douglas, Arizona, I used my birth name, George Kuri, which was also the name on my school transfer. However, when my mom enrolled me at Breed Street Elementary School, she requested that I be enrolled with the last name Hatcher, her married name. When I met Pi, I introduced myself by saying, "My name is George Hatcher," as we shook hands. "My name is Pi."

* * *

After helping Pi with his homework that afternoon, I became the soft touch that the tough guys came to for homework help. Little by little, I befriended them all. It was good for my health. We were just kids. None of us was older than eleven.

My mother gave me a two-dollar weekly allowance to clean the house and heat up the food she had prepared the night before. Our landlord paid me five a month to water the grass and clean the driveway. Two tenants paid me a quarter[1] once a week to wash their cars. A few extra bucks came from the other tenants for burning their trash in the incinerator, which I would have done for free because lighting a fire in the incinerator was a challenge to keep from wasting a lot of matches.

Like in Douglas, I had money in my pocket.

I saved up and bought a used bike for five dollars. It cost another five to get it working. Once I had a way to get around, I got a job delivering the Times-Mirror.

Delivering papers in LA was very different from Douglas. The LA route covered more than two miles, and the hills were steep. I got a real workout pedaling up every morning. Going down was another story.

After four months, I made a deal with a boy in school to pay me ten dollars to take over my route. I got a new Schwinn and went to work for the Herald on an afternoon route. I was making money, but not enough.

One day I told Pi about an idea I had.

"Hey, man, want to do some yard work with me on

---

1. $.25 in 1952 would be $2.42 in 2020

weekends? I'm thinking of buying a power lawnmower and going into business. I'll cut you in for thirty percent."

Pi had dimples, and he smiled when he was content and also when he was pissed off. I'd watch his expression like a hawk, but when he smiled, it could go either way.

"What's thirty percent, man?"

"For every dollar we get, you get thirty cents. After all, I'm the one going to buy the lawnmower. Are you interested?"

"Sounds like a rip-off," Pi said.

"Okay, I'll give you thirty-two percent."

"You mean thirty-two cents on a dollar?"

"Yeah. Are you interested?"

"What if the person has their own lawnmower, and we don't use yours?"

"Don't get complicated," I said. "Thirty-two percent is a good deal."

"All right, I'll try it. But you're ripping me off. I know you are."

Pi, whose real name was Joe, played a significant role in boosting my popularity at school. Although I never became a member of the gang, Joe and I were inseparable. With him by my side, nobody messed with me. I became a neutral figure, someone that all the kids trusted and sought advice from. They would come to me with various issues, including problems with other gangs.

Acting as a go-between, I took on the responsibility of maintaining peace within the school. Despite Joe's persistent attempts to persuade me, I stood firm in my decision not to join the gang.

"Become one of us," he'd say.

And I would say, "I am. We are all friends."

Then one day, he admitted, "I'm glad you're not in the gang. I think we're better this way."

"We'll always be friends, Joe."

"You're the only person who calls me 'Joe.'"

"So what?"

"Sounds pretty good," he said with a loud laugh. "Don't go calling me 'Joe' in front of the boys."

But I did, and he never stopped me.

Eventually, I sold my second paper route to another friend and worked yards every day. I bought more tools and eventually agreed to give Pi forty percent. Some places where we did the lawns wanted a car to be washed. We charged thirty cents for that. The hardware store owner told me it was easier to dry a car with a chamois and leave no streaks, so I bought two chamois. Working together and hanging out, Pi and I were on the road to becoming good friends. He swore that he couldn't trust anyone who wasn't a member of his gang, but me, he was coming to trust.

My share was more than I could make on my paper route in a whole month. Fifteen dollars a week was about a third of what my mom earned. One day after we split the weekly take, Pi agreed we were going to get rich.

Pi admitted he never worked in his whole life. I, on the other hand, started early.

I heard a salesman tell Leonard he could buy anything he wanted with his excellent credit and take up to three years to pay in small monthly payments. The store was Dearden's on 7th & Main in downtown Los Angeles. Our apartment's dingy furniture came with the apartment. Once I knew it was possible, I pestered my parents to buy new for the whole place, including a brand-new TV with a twenty-one-inch screen. My dad made a deal with the owner of the apartment, who owned the furniture. He told my dad to donate it to the Salvation Army if he promised to stay at least two more years as a tenant. The deal was done. Hands were shaken. New furniture came, and the place looked marvelous.

My girl Cathy Reader, a pretty blonde with a pageboy, attended a Lutheran private school, so I only saw her after school and only if I was free from work. She lived two blocks away on my street. She roller-skated to my house, and when she was ready to leave, I accompanied her home, both of us on skates. It was a big deal to roller-skate holding hands on the sidewalk, and exciting when she let me kiss her goodnight.

* * *

I told my mother I'd come up with part of the monthly payment and bought her a Singer electric sewing machine. I was proud of the apartment with the new furniture, TV, and sewing machine.

As one of the few kids at school who had a TV, a brand new one at that, I had a lot of visitors in the early evenings after finishing my gardening jobs. The space was tight. If my parents were around, they sat on the sofa and cushioned chairs. The guys and I sat on the floor on a new rug that was almost the size of the living room. Everyone left their shoes outside. The shoe thing was my rule.

My parents were easygoing. They didn't mind sharing the television with my flock of friends, but what we wanted to watch and what my parents liked to watch wasn't the same thing.

"We got to find a better meeting place than my living room," I told Pi.

"You ain't using the garage," Pi said.

Each apartment had a big garage. We had no car to put in there, so we started a collection to buy a TV.

"Why don't we just steal one at Sears?" one of the guys said.

Two others were all for it.

"We're not stealing a TV," Pi said.

"We need more bucks than we got from your boys," I told Pi. "How about we ask Ramon and Mickey's boys to pitch in, and they can come over when they want?"

"They ain't part of the gang, man."

Pi resisted.

"So what? They're in the neighborhood, and you've been at peace."

It took some persuasion, but with the lure of a television, Pi agreed.

He was a tough eleven-year-old.

The two gangs pitched in. Pi had a talk with the leaders.

"Ain't going to be any fights or bullshit over at the clubhouse," he told them, "or they'll be some heads cracked. Got it?"

We bought extension cords to run electricity from my apartment to the garage set back far from the back door. It was a lot of extension cords.

Things were peaceful until girls started coming over. Tempers got short. Nerves frayed. The hours were great for Pi and me, but not the best for everyone else. My garage didn't open up until Pi and I finished doing our gardening and car washes. Summers, Los Angeles gets dark after eight in the evening. It was late, but the girls would come and stay as long as the sunlight lasted. Anyway, girls became a problem, starting like this:

"Motha-fucker, that's my girl you got your slimy hands on!" one of Mickey's gang shouted. Then all of Mickey's gang would chime in.

"Fuck you, man," Pi's boys said. "We'll slap you around and see whose girl she is."

Pi stepped in, shoved the girl aside, and slapped the mouthy gang members.

"Let's step across the street and settle this!" Pi yelled, his face flushed and grim.

"Hey Pi," I said, "My parents are in the living room watching TV in direct view of the park. They don't need to see anybody not getting along."

The girl that caused the issue said, "Let's watch some TV and knock this shit off. No fighting."

Pi shrugged. "She right," he said.

Everyone settled in the chair or on a bench or wood box they kept in my garage to sit on.

Pi was husky and tough. I admired how he handled himself. He was nothing if not a natural leader. Members of his gang would fool around, and he'd let them punch his stomach and chest. I don't know where the muscle came from except maybe sit-ups and pushups. Eleven-year-old kids don't usually work out that way. Pi was way ahead of us. I believe he had an influence on me. I started doing pushups, and started arm-wrestling with him, but he was too strong. In time, I got better. In time I would get strong so that I could get punched and laugh away the impact.

* * *

I started thinking that my dad Leonard should have a car, so he didn't have to take the bus or streetcar after a long workday. He had seen a Ford he liked. We talked about it over dinner sometimes.

"I like the car," my dad said. "I don't need it to be new, and seven hundred down isn't the only problem. We have to finish paying off the furniture, and-."

"But you have excellent credit, and you can get anything you want."

"I know, son. But a car payment and a furniture payment are more than we can afford right now."

I was too young to drive, but once the idea of having a car got in my head, the dream haunted me. There had to be a way to get enough money to pay off the furniture and car balances. After school the next day, I told Joe to finish the gardening jobs by himself. I went to Bank of America, where I kept my savings account.

The receptionist looked at me funny when I asked to see

someone about a loan, but she told me to take a seat and that a Mr. Holmberg would see me.

An older man, very composed and very distinguished looking, wearing a three-piece suit and glasses, came out to see me, looking exactly like I would have expected a banker to look. What there was of his hair was dark and short, and he was clean-shaven. He could have played a professional man in a magazine advertisement. That's how banker-like he looked. Nothing about him called attention to itself.

"I understand you want to see me about a loan," Mr. Holmberg said.

As he shook my hand, he was grinning. He was probably wondering what a kid like me was doing conducting business by himself in a bank.

I explained that the loan was really for my parents, who worked all day and couldn't come in for information. I was cool as a cucumber. It never occurred to me to be nervous. I guess I got this way because my mother always had me translate and be the middleman in any situation that involved filling out forms.

Mr. Holmberg led me past four desks out in the open, and into his office. It was a bank office like any other those days, no windows, four walls, metal and wood furniture, a small room with a desk, chair, phone, and pictures of former President Harry Truman and President Dwight D Eisenhower on the wall. There was a family picture standing framed on his desk. I knew he had to be important to have an office with walls. I sat in a hard wooden chair with arms and wheels and earnestly told him the whole story about the furniture loan, the car we wished to buy, and where my parents worked. He listened attentively. He was impressed when I showed him my savings passbook with a balance of three hundred eighty-six dollars.

"How old are you, son?"

"Almost twelve."

"I have a boy. He's twelve."

"Does he have a job?"

"No, not yet."

"Maybe I can find him one."

Mr. Holmberg smiled broadly. "I'll tell him," he said. He handed me a credit application for my parents to fill out and walked me to the front door with his arm around my shoulders like I was his son or someone special.

Afraid that my parents might not want to go to the trouble of applying for the loan, I filled out the credit application myself and took it back to Mr. Holmberg the next day. If their credit checked out okay, he said he could loan them between one thousand to two thousand dollars with a payment of about $40 dollars a month - only six dollars more than the furniture payments. I left the bank feeling that we might just get the car.

Leonard was a busy man, maintaining elevators of a fifteen-story building on 9th & Broadway. It was tedious work and maybe even dangerous. He didn't speak Spanish. My mom was getting English lessons from a nun at St Mary's School a couple times a week. Leonard wanted my mom to be happy, and the two of them gave me way too much authority to run a lot of their lives. I didn't object at all.

Language barrier or not, my mother and Leonard got along great. I don't know how, but they communicated. They cooked together on weekends. My mom prepared dinner before she left every day, and I was charged with getting it in the oven or whatever. I put dinner in the oven, they got home from work, and we ate.

After dinner, I told my parents about going to the bank. Leonard scratched his head, maybe in disbelief, but they went back with me to the bank that Friday. Mr. Holmberg treated me like we were old friends. After that, I made a point to see Mr. Holmberg each time I made a deposit. My dad said he would take the smaller loan and get a used car. Finding a car took a week. Then, bingo, my dad had wheels. A black Ford. It looked new to me. He parked it the back of our apartment but not in the garage.

On Christmas Eve day, I gave Mr. Holmberg a bottle of Old Spice aftershave. He handed me an envelope with a fifty-dollar savings bond inside.

As I passed his secretary on my way out, she said, "By the way, George, stop by my house one of these days and give me an estimate to do my lawn."

"Give me the address, and I'll go take care of it for a month, free of charge. After that, we'll talk if you like the work."

"You're quite a businessman," she said, writing down her address.

"Merry Christmas," I said.

Chapter 4
Hollenbeck Junior High

In January, I entered Hollenbeck Junior High School, which was bigger and had a tougher rep than elementary school. I was twelve. Students at Hollenbeck were Mexican, African American, and more than a third were Japanese. For the most part, the Japanese came from families that owned businesses and were well dressed and did not join gangs. In other parts of Los Angeles there were many Asian gangs, but not where I was, and not at Hollenbeck when I was there. The new school meant more homework, more activities, and less time free for work. The groups stopped coming over. I studied hard and told Pi I was only going to work weekends. Weekends could make me enough to help at home and take care of my needs, although I wouldn't be able to save.

I saw less of Pi. My new friends from school weren't gang members. Pi noticed the change but understood. We were friends but friends with different goals. When I did see him, he would make a big deal in front of the boys. His gang was the most powerful of all the gangs at Hollenbeck. I stayed neutral, a friend to all sides. It wasn't easy.

* * *

"Got a big war coming up at the park tomorrow," Pi said one morning on the way to school.

"How come you don't look worried, then?"

"Cause them black dudes ain't got shit over us. We'll kill em."

He could've been right, but I hoped not.

"Your war should be a fistfight. Clubs and chains and all that shit don't prove anything. It leads to guns when everyone gets pissed, and people die, and families cry, and the cops come and take everybody away. A real challenge should be with bare knuckles and guts. You see what guys are really made of that way."

He hitched up his chinos at the crotch.

"You should be in the movies," he said. "Good thing we're friends."

"Yeah, good thing."

"We could beat them bare knuckles, but that fuckin' Hank won't go for it. So, fuck it."

"I thought you were the king on campus, Pi. What gives, man? You ain't got enough pull to force that kind of fight?"

"I ain't asking that motha a damn thing."

Later that afternoon, I made it my business to catch up with Hank. Hank was a big kid, more muscle than flab, and towered over me. Size is sometimes a lot of the reason guys like Hank and Pi end up in charge. Hank towered over most people. He flashed his familiar wide, toothy grin. He had a different kind of chip on his shoulder than Pi did.

"You know I don't get involved in these wars, Hank. But if you're smart, you should do something different on this one. I got an idea."

"Tell me, man."

In the end, he agreed, providing I would be responsible for Pi's boys not violating the ground rules.

Pi was incredulous. "I can't believe the mothas agreed."

I told Pi, "Those mothas will kill me if you go crazy and pull out weapons. So, keep it in mind, friend."

He brushed a finger under his nose, sniffing at the idea. "It would serve you right for butting in."

* * *

It was one of those ugly LA days in the height of winter when it looked like the threat of rain that would never come. The park was a dirty disaster area, overgrown grass, glass on the ground, walls sprayed with graffiti. Garbage, beer bottles, and shell casings littered the park. The lake was grimy, and most of the grass was dry and dead and unkempt. The park was a wreck, but it was our wreck, and the chosen site for the showdown.

The gangs began to arrive.

"Everyone check your stuff in with me," I said. "All of it."

The fight began. It was not a turf fight. It was a blow-off-steam fight. A turf fight or a get-even fight would have been spontaneous. No advance planning would have occurred.

As soon as Hank and Pi squared off, everyone jumped in. I was scared for all of us. Next to me was a gunnysack filled with knives, screwdrivers, clubs, glass bottles, rolls of change, brass knuckles, and baseball bats. Even if I wasn't in it, I was taking a chance by just being there. If the cops showed, they'd haul in everybody, and especially me, with custody of all the weapons. In the end, no one was badly hurt. No cops showed up.

I'm uncertain about why I took such a risk, perhaps I thought I could talk my way out of trouble if the police had shown up. In my mind, I had intervened to prevent a potentially harmful situation.

Pi came out of the brawl sweating, and only a few scratches. He was amazing. Hank didn't look hurt either. Their soldiers, well, that was a different story.

My first girlfriend at Hollenbeck was Patty Nisei. Patty was pretty, and Japanese, and lived with her mother and brother in City Terrace. Her father had gone to Japan on business five years before and then wrote to say he was never coming back. Her mother was a punch-press operator for a hardware manufacturer and managed to make her mortgage payment and still dress Patty in nice clothes. Patty took the bus from school to City Terrace, where she lived.

Patty was in all my classes except physical education. I had started to meet up with her during recess, and we exchanged some crazy notes in our classes. At lunch, we had grilled cheese and sat together. I asked her, "How many boyfriends do you have?"

Her smile was perfect.

"How many girlfriends do you have?" she replied.

"Come over," she invited after school before she caught her bus.

"I do yard work and wash cars. It would have to be after dinner."

I figured it was too late and that her mother would disapprove.

"I'm up late. It's okay," she said. "My mom won't mind. We're late people."

"Are you sure?"

"Here's the address," she said, writing it on a sheet of paper from her three-ring binder. "Think you can find it?"

"I used to deliver newspapers. I know my way around City Terrace."

Patty said, "Awesome."

Anyway, we barely knew each other, and she was asking me to come over. "I can come earlier if I can bring my homework," I said.

"Awesome," she said.

I loved the way she said awesome.

I had a quick dinner at home.

"Junior High is not easy. I am going to a friend's house to do my homework," I said. "She lives far, all the way in City Terrace."

They were okay with it. I had a key to the front door, and I knew they went to bed early.

I pedaled my bike up the winding hills and down the slopes to City Terrace, and I found the house on Stone Street. I got there at six.

I met her mother, Thelma, and her little brother, Steve. Her mom smiled a lot like Patty did, and they had the same kind of grin. They were friendly as all heck. Off their living room, their balcony had a fantastic view of downtown Los Angeles.

"I see all the hills I had to take on to get here," I said.

"I'm glad you came over," Patty said. "I'm sorry about the hills."

We sat at a table outside on the balcony and worked on homework. It took a while to get the hang of how we should do it since we had identical work. When we were done, it was dark, and we went inside.

"Are you in a hurry? Do you want to watch TV?"

"I'm good if you are," I said.

"I'll get us a coke."

I followed her into her room, and she shut the door with her hip because she carried a couple of glass coke bottles in her hands. A TV was in her bedroom. There was also a small desk with a lamp and chair, and another chair near her bed. Her bedspread was colorful and impressive, and her room was as cool as any teenager's room I had ever seen. She had a window with a view of the balcony we had been on. She turned off the overhead light and left the lamp next to her bed on.

Like it was no big deal, Patty propped up two pillows against the headboard and sat down. I sat on the wood chair.

"Come over here," she said. "You can't watch TV from there."

She patted a spot next to her.

"Are you sure?"

"Kick your shoes off and get up here. It's okay. You sure aren't shy at school. You joke around with every girl in all our classes."

I got on the bed.

"Not true, I only have eyes for you."

"I'm supposed to believe that?" she giggled.

So, we were watching something like I Love Lucy, Dragnet, or Gunsmoke. We were talking more than watching. I heard a knock on the door, which made my heart leap, and I almost jumped off the bed. Patty touched my arm.

"Relax," she smiled.

Her mom came in and handed us a bowl of nuts.

"Japanese nuts," she said and left.

Patty was my age. I was nervous and didn't understand how she could be so calm. I'd never been in a bed with a girl before. We were dressed. She was barefoot. I had my socks on. Good thing I changed them after my gardening work before dinner.

At nine, I told her good night. She walked me to the front door.

"Thanks for having me over," I said.

"Are you going to leave without kissing me?"

I remembered Valita when she kissed me in the dark garage with two cars sitting there, and then my hand was guided to the spot. I remembered the scent of her.

"Well?" Patty put her hands on her hips.

I didn't hug her or anything. I moved my face close, and our lips met quickly.

I stared at her. Her eyes were closed.

She said, "Well."

I kissed her again, and our lips touched longer this time.

I pedaled my bike uphill and flew down. I let go of the handlebars and screamed out loud.

Screamed just for the noise. Whoops of joy. And some words too. "Love that girl!" at the top of my lungs, racing downhill at half-past nine, probably disturbing all the people in the houses I passed between City Terrace and St. Louis Street.

I kept thinking about the kiss. Twice!

When I let myself in at home, I found my parents were asleep. I took the rollaway out quietly, and opened it up. It was already made up. I undressed and got cozy, closed my eyes, but my brain was still racing downhill and moving faster than it should have been for my age. I thought I had to be dreaming. I thought about the kisses again. I thought about Valita.

In the eighth grade, the counselor messed things up. We had only three classes together. We both took student government. I dug that class. The teacher was a tall, middle-aged guy with a senator's gift for public speaking. I got into parliamentary procedure and was appointed class parliamentarian. When there was a dispute about the procedure, it was up to me to set out the proper way to present something, say something, etc. If I didn't have the answer, the teacher stepped in. Then I knew the next time.

I had lunch with Patty daily unless she met up with her girlfriends or I was on the hunt with other girls I liked.

"I love the way you talk in class," Patty said. "You're so smart, George."

"I'm not smart. You're the one who is smart."

She had a brain for math and algebra.

There were very pretty girls at school. I did my share of flirting. By the ninth grade, instead of hanging out at Patty's house on Friday, we went to our school's Friday night dances. Seventh and eighth-grade students had their own dance room. We ninth graders had a revolving mirror ball and color spotlights illuminating the ceiling. I danced the slow dances with as many girls as wanted to dance.

Patty was like a magnet. I looked forward to being with her, and I saw her every night and every day. We continued working together on our homework.

"I noticed you danced to every tune, fast and slow," I told her during our homework time.

"I noticed you did pretty good yourself," she replied.

"I don't mind slow. The other, I only do when I'm in a spot."

"I can teach you," she assured me. And she did. I mentioned to her that a long time ago, Pi had attempted to teach me the bebop. Despite his size, he was an impressive dancer.

We always found something to do after homework.

"Is your mom complaining about your being out every day like this?"

I said, "Not yet, but eventually, she'll get around to it."

"Tell her you have a night job," Patty suggested.

"A night job? And I'm in school?" I laughed, and she did too.

I cut back gardening and washing cars to weekends. That way, I could get to Patty's earlier each day, do our homework, fool around, and get home earlier than before. We also had drama together and had parts in a couple of plays. I liked Miss Mitchell, the drama teacher. Patty and I practiced lines together. The plays were great fun despite taking so much time away from everything else. Patty said I got a big standing ovation, but all I heard was clapping. After that, everybody at school knew my name. Drama class didn't interfere with work. Pi made more money by doing the weekday work with one or two of his gang associates. He was happy. On weekends, I did it all and kept all the money, our new deal. After work on Saturday and Sunday, I'd shower and head to Patty's.

Patty's Mom Thelma gave me presents- shirts, novelty t-shirts, random stuff.

"I feel bad accepting gifts like this," I told her mom.

"It is my pleasure," Thelma said. "It's a tradition when you like someone the way we like you to give gifts."

"Thank you, I love everything, but please don't give me so much."

I knew Patty's father in Japan never sent a dime to her mom, and it made me feel bad that she spent money on me.

Patty and I were pulling off A's. Helping each other made making the grade so much easier. We rushed through homework to get to other things. At first, 'other things' was necking, then it became heavy petting.

"You need to lock the door," I said.

"Okay, I will, but my mom will not walk in, ever."

"Yeah, but what about your brother?"

"Okay," she said. "Okay."

Patty and I learned about massage decades before the Joy of Sex popularized it decades later. Patty would work on my back and legs while I was on my stomach, and then I would reciprocate by massaging the same areas on her.

Eventually, we incorporated more body parts into our massage routine.

Patty's figure continued to improve beneath the clothes she wore to school. She claimed that at age ten, puberty struck. It happened a year before I did. Other guys were circling her like preying hawks. Patty and I would yoyo-split up and then get back together, just like any couple who see each other too frequently.

During our breakups, we still talked on the phone.

"Did he leave?" I asked.

"Yes."

"Did you give him a massage?"

"Did you give Aida a massage?"

I laughed, and she laughed.

"I miss you," I said.

"You don't miss me. I saw you kissing Aida at nutrition, and you were with Elena at lunch."

"Oh, so you noticed?"

"I'm going to bed," she said.

"Me too."

* * *

Around town, I noticed a bicycle with the Red Arrow name on it, and a young guy wearing a blue hat. I figured it might be fun, and I could make money. At the start of the two-week spring break, I applied and bang - I had a job at Red Arrow Messenger Service in downtown Los Angeles. I started delivering envelopes to business offices and department stores located in downtown Los Angeles DTLA. United Parcel Services owned the delivery company. I worked eight hours a day every day, and I was never late. It was a lot of work but fun. I got to ride around on a bike and get paid for it. I used their bikes, had to wear a hat with their logo, and I got tips. While working, I left the bike in front of wherever I was delivering, and no one bothered it because signs on both sides of the bike displayed Red Arrow Messenger.

I promised the Red Arrow manager that I would return to work on summer break. He told me he would have a job open for me. I don't think I had a work permit. I don't think it mattered back then.

Patty would break up with her boyfriend, and I would break up with the girl I was with and we wasted no time getting back together.

"Let's not break up for a while," Patty said.

"Deal. I miss you like crazy when we're apart."

Patty's brother was laid back. He always looked at me like I was a dud. I think he was jealous that his mom gave me presents, and I wondered if he got any. Like Patty, he was always in nice clothes, even at home, the only place I saw him.

Thelma hugged me. "I'm glad to see you," she said. "I don't like her other friends."

"Oh, mom, stop it," Patty said.

Patty would kiss me lightly on the cheek. That's what I got in front of her mom.

* * *

When we were in the bedroom, and the door was locked, Patty and I went at each other. At thirteen, we almost got as far as adults go, but not all the way. Patty didn't have a repressed bone in her body and did whatever she wanted freely, but when I asked her to turn on the light and stand there so I could see her body, she got shy.

We chuckled over everything. Joyful mischievous teenagers.

* * *

The last day of school was almost like a party. We turned in our books. Exams were done. Some of the teachers gave us our grades. Miss Mitchell, the blonde teacher from drama, wrote on my annual to send her a dozen red roses when I made my first million dollars.

I did that.

* * *

When summer arrived, I was ready to return to Red Arrow Messenger, but my stepdad offered to help me get something better than riding on a bike all day. I said, fine. In the fifteen-story building where he worked, all the tenants were designers with showrooms of women's fashion, where retail stores shop for women's clothes. He talked to William, a women's dress distributor, and William hired me to work at Moss Fashions.

William's showroom was big, with racks filled with dresses, jackets, coats. You name it, they had it. Gus ran William's shipping department, the only employee working there. Gus was a tall black guy who should have gone out for basketball. Gus and I would push a clothes rack filled with what the department store had ordered, and we delivered it to big stores like Bullocks, May Company, Robinsons, The Broadway and to small stores, too. Sometimes business was so good for William that he sold out, and his racks were empty awaiting shipments.

The racks were long steel racks with wheels. Gus and I would cover the merchandise and zipper it up in covers bearing the company's big logo.

Most times for lunch. I would meet up with my stepdad at the engineering office building, his office at the top of the building. If an electrical panel or something went bad, my dad went down and fixed it. If one of the four elevators had a problem, my dad took care of it. If it was a plumbing issue, he called a plumber. He didn't mess around with plumbing.

For lunch, we'd go to the Orpheum Theatre Eatery, which was immediately next door. I loved their hamburgers. I always tried to pay for lunch, but my dad wouldn't let me.

When I got off an hour after he went home, I rode the streetcar that ran down Broadway, then turned on 1st Street and headed toward East Los Angeles. Japan town was right after the turn on 1st Street, where a lot of my friends' parents had businesses. It was not like Chinatown where you came to the carnival. These were newspaper companies, pharmacies, travel agencies, sign painters, flower shops, grocery stores specializing in Japanese foods, and the like.

My stop was Chicago Street, where I got off and walked three blocks to the apartment. I wanted to take my bike to work, but there was no place to put it around that building. I couldn't wait to turn sixteen, get a driver's license, and buy a car. I still had my savings account at Mr. Holmberg's bank and I planned to use the money to buy a car in cash or to put a down payment on it.

In the 9th grade, I ran for boy's student body vice president, and Patty ran for girl's student body vice president. My former girlfriend, Aida, ran for student body president. Since we were already in student government class, we knew about campaigns. Pi, his friends, and my other best friend Kenji and his friends worked on banners, posters, and signs for me. Patty also had a lot of support.

Aida was so popular she could have made it without a campaign. The three of us won. That put us in student government, for another semester. I loved it. I actually loved school, so what happened later remains a mystery to me.

* * *

Patty and I were in her bedroom.

"I need to find a good job," I said. "I want to buy a car the day I turn sixteen."

"Okay," she said.

"Why does your mother do so much for me?"

We were lying on the top bedspread, both of us staring at the ceiling, and Patty kissed me.

"She's just being nice to her future son-in-law."

I kissed her back, but my brain fixed on that big word, son-in-law. I was fourteen. We both lay back down and resumed contemplating the nipple-shaped light fixture in the center of the grainy white plaster ceiling. The shadow it cast got lighter and more distorted as it slowly got darker outside and in.

"She wants us to get married someday?" I asked.

"Boy, does she."

"How do you feel about it?"

I wondered whether she'd grow up to look like her mother. I won't say her mother wasn't pretty, but she had left fourteen behind a long time ago. Marriage was a lifetime away, impossible to picture. I couldn't see myself as a man. I couldn't see Patty as all grown-up. I sure couldn't see myself married, not even to Aida, who was a future Miss America.

"I'm like you, George. It's years away. Life is just beginning."

I snuggled up to her. "I noticed your breasts are getting nicer."

"Nicer?"

"They've always been nice, but I noticed how they looked with the sweater you had on today."

Patty loved to tease. "Tell me how they looked."

"I could see your nipples."

"Did you get hard?"

"I did." I touched her breasts. "Let me see."

That night we left the lamp on, and I explored the body I had been touching for months and months. She did the same. Her hand was on my thing. She always had a hand on it when we were in bed, no matter what we were doing, unless she was massaging me.

"Let's not break up for a while," I teased. "I like what I see."

She gave me a playful squeeze.

"Ouch."

We kissed, our hands roamed, and we got very hot and bothered.

Later she said, "Let's always be best friends, no matter what happens."

I looked at her like she was crazy to think we would someday not be friends. "That's a given, Patty, always and forever. Even when we split up, we're on the phone talking to each other. That's never going to change."

We did a pinky squeeze. We kissed.

"I love the way you talk," she said.

"I love the way you are," I said.

It wasn't planned. It just happened. Totally dumb to do it with no protection, but our bodies were smoking with heat.

"We need to vent the room in case your mom wants in," I said, thinking about the scent Valita had left in my brain years back. Now the scent permeated the bedroom.

"You are such a worrier," she said.

Afterwards, Patty said, "It's about time. We waited so long. Any regrets?"

"You have to be kidding," I said. "No regrets. I loved it."

"I loved it, too," she said. "I hope we didn't just make a baby."

We stared at the ceiling for a minute, breathing quietly.

Patty asked, "Is this when you go home, or do you want to do it again?"

Her hands found me, making it clear which way she wanted to vote.

"I'm in," I said. "I only need a little help from you."

Pretty soon, we were laughing and rolling around again. It was so easy at that age to laugh about anything.

* * *

I gave a pretty good speech at graduation. Since Aida was student body president, she had to speak too, and she did great. Patty's speech was inspiring. I told her she should save it for high school graduation because it was that good. Pi and most of his gang pulled it off and graduated when we did. Several friends from his gang couldn't make it because they were in juvenile hall. We transferred to Roosevelt High School, one block from Hollenbeck Junior High.

* * *

I was hired at a large drugstore not far from school. It was not as big as a CVS of today, but it had a lot of merchandise. My job was to deliver prescriptions after school. With tips, I made more money than any of my jobs before, plus I got a discount on anything I purchased.

Sometimes it was too late to head out from the drugstore to City Terrace on a bicycle. Anyway, Patty would call me, or I would call her late at night when everyone was asleep. We talked and talked. Sometimes I would fall asleep or she would. I only had one class with her in the 10th grade at Roosevelt High.

Chapter 5
A New Job

When I finished the pharmacy deliveries, I'd cut up empty merchandise cartons in the stockroom and carry them out to the rubbish bins. When there was free time, the owner would have me help at the front register. At first, I bagged purchases. Little by little, I started working the cash register. I got the hang of it.

The boss observed me at work as he filled prescriptions from across the store in the back. Mr. Schultz was a pharmacist. It was busy, sometimes with all three pharmacists on duty at the same time. The lady that worked the pharmacy prescription counter also rang up cosmetics right next to that department.

One day the owner asked if I wanted to work the front register and stock the liquor department and sundries.

"If you want to do this, I'll give you a raise, and I'll hire someone else to do deliveries," he said.

"I'd like that," I said.

"You're going to be working more hours. If this interferes with your schoolwork, we can leave you where you are. School comes first."

"I can handle both," I said.

My being bilingual helped. I advanced to assistant cashier and was assigned to the sundry counter that included bottled liquor. Back then, minors could sell liquor as long as it was sealed. That register rang up a whole bunch of sales, a lot of it liquor, developing photographs and film.

The girl I assisted was a strikingly beautiful twenty-two-year-old redhead named Christine. I was smitten, but she treated me like the kid I was. She flirted with me occasionally, but she laughed off the advances I made. It's not like we hadn't met before I was working there. But now, I was a cashier, and she was still laughing off my advances. She still flirted with me.

"You should be nice to me," I'd say. "Before I was put here you did all this work on your own." That would get a smile from her. She was so pretty.

I became infatuated with Christine, and she consumed a significant portion of my thoughts. After several weeks, I began to notice that she was engaged in a cunning scheme involving the cash register. Instead of individually ringing up each item for a customer, she would jot down a list of items on a sheet of paper. Then, she would collect the money from the customer and enter a lower total into the cash register or perform a 'no sale' transaction. This allowed her to pocket some of the cash without raising suspicion. Whenever customers came to pick up their photos, they would often get engrossed in examining the pictures, oblivious to the cash register. To open the cash drawer, she would either perform a 'no sale' transaction or enter a sale of a small amount. It was a clever tactic. All transactions were conducted in cash or check. Credit cards were not accepted.

Frequently, a regular customer would come in and purchase a bottle of liquor directly from the shelf, bypassing the line. They would place a bill on the counter and wave to Christine, indicating that they were in a hurry. Although the money would go into the cash register, Christine wouldn't ring up the full amount or would enter a lower price. For example, if the liquor cost $4.75 and the customer placed a five-dollar bill on the counter, Christine would only ring up $1.75 and make a mental or written note that she had three dollars coming off that sale. I assumed that she kept track of these discrepancies, and at the end of the day, when she counted the cash, she would take the amount that had not been properly rung up from the register.

I confirmed my suspicions by retrieving a piece of paper from the wastebasket and comparing it to the sales recorded on the cash register. Once I had figured it out, I observed her closely and noticed that she did it frequently. She was incredibly quick, like a firecracker. A beautiful girl like her could get away with anything.

Whenever they could steal a moment away from the pharmacy counter in the back, the owner and other pharmacists would come up and chat with her, undoubtedly hoping for various unsavory things. Male customers would gawk at her instead of paying attention to the items she rang up on the cash register. There was no way they would notice how much she rang up for their purchases. She must have been pocketing an easy fifty dollars or more a day, which explained how she could afford stylish attire and drive a new Impala that cost two thousand dollars. Fifty dollars was a substantial sum.

I didn't say anything to her right off. I waited. But eventually, I did bring it up.

"Christi, I think we should talk about you cutting me in on your little side business."

She laughed at me, called me a snoopy squirt, and told me to bug off. Until then, she seemed to like me, flirted, laughed with me. When I brought up her little plan, then all of a sudden, she wanted to squash me like a bug.

I pushed my luck.

"If you won't cut me in, I may consider taking it in trade. What is going to be, money or trade? What's my silence worth?"

What I got from her was a slap. It burned. It pissed me off, but I stayed cool.

"You aren't old enough to get it up," she said with a nasty frown. She laughed.

* * *

We continued to work together. After a day or so it was like nothing had ever happened. Sometimes when we were busy and trying to work around each other with one register, she would grind her fine ass against me. I was not imagining it.

One day, I told her that the owner asked me if I had noticed anything strange about how she handled the register. Christine's face turned white. It thrilled me to see her as worried as she looked. It was payback for the slap.

"What did you tell him?" she asked.

"I covered for you and acted really surprised. I told him there was no way you were taking money."

Christine smiled, relief flooding her face. She actually kissed me. A peck on my cheek.

"You'd better stay cool for a while, Christine," I advised solemnly.

She nodded.

"I will, I will."

I could almost hear the gears whirring in her head. I held my breath.

"Maybe you and I can make a deal of some kind, Georgie."

She brushed back the mane of flaming hair then allowed it to fall forward. She batted her big, brown eyes at me.

"Maybe we'll go somewhere after work and discuss this in private," she said with a coquettish grin.

The evening dragged on as I waited in anticipation. What I had told her was a lie, of course. Mr. Schultz loved Christine. As far as I knew, he never suspected her of wrongdoing. If he had, why on earth would he ever turn to me?

After work, Christine drove us to a motel. I waited in the car while she checked in. My hands were wet with anticipation, but I didn't want to let on that I was nervous. I was a little insecure about being seen walking into a motel with a tall, gorgeous woman eight years older than me. She came out with a key and parked right in front of the room. I wasn't even sure what we would be doing in the hotel. After all, I didn't know Christine outside the drugstore.

It didn't take long to figure it out. Christine didn't mess around or waste time. I was feeling shy, and she was laughing at me the whole time she undressed. She was naked when she pulled the blanket down to the foot of the bed and got on top of the hopefully clean sheets. I was so worked up I hadn't digested the centerfold that was right there with me.

I hung back and watched nervously. I had seen Patty naked. There was no part of her body I hadn't visited in the dark. This was not Patty. I was in a motel with

Christine, the first adult woman I had ever seen totally naked. She was the goddess of Motel 6, leggy and voluptuous. No woman to compare had ever been on that bed.

She told me to take off my clothes.

I didn't want to disappoint her, but I was paralyzed. I couldn't budge.

"What's the matter, Georgie? You got a little thing?"

"It's not little," I said.

"Then why don't you take off your clothes?"

"I will. I just have to get used to this is all."

"You talked about a trade. I thought for sure you were ready."

"I'm up for it if you turn off the lights." I thought of Patty. She liked it dark. With her I wanted the lights on. With Christine, I wanted the lights out.

"No, Georgie. Grownups don't do it in the dark."

She was laughing at me again. I was frozen with embarrassment. She got off the bed. I was eager but getting me undressed with the lights on was a wrestling match.

She was a hurricane of what we called in junior high Russian hands and Roman fingers because her hands were rushing and roaming all over the place. When my clothes were flung across the room, and I was finally standing in front of her completely nude, I almost panicked.

At least she stopped laughing.

"You're right, Georgie. It's not little."

She embraced me tightly, planting a kiss on my lips that surpassed any previous experience. As we tumbled onto the bed, her warm breath mingled with mine, igniting a surge of excitement within me. The intoxicating aroma of her presence pushed me beyond the brink of pleasure.

"I'll teach you a thing or two," she whispered. "Try to relax. I don't bite. Much."

My embarrassment dissolved.

"We'll start with oral sex," she said.

That was a first for me. She guided my face downward and explained what she wanted. I couldn't back out. Then my head was filled with the scent of her, like the scent I had been carrying for years of Valita when she put my hand on her.

I did what she asked. She was ecstatic. She moaned and bucked. Her passion and reaction made me so excited that I forgot all about being nervous. She didn't want me to stop. After she said, "I came four times. I don't believe for a second this was your first time."

She came four times, but I didn't ask her to explain. I was aware of how a man reached his peak, but I was completely clueless about how a lady got off.

Before leaving the motel I heard myself tell her that our boss had not asked me about her. She turned red as a tomato. We were dressed and ready to go out the door. Christine sat on the edge of the bed and stared up at me. "You creep!"

* * *

From that memorable night onwards, we transformed into co-conspirators, joining forces to subtly pilfer from the workplace cash register. She was an excellent mentor in matters of intimacy and equally adept at the art of subtle theft. There were days when our illicit gains were less, but on average, we did quite well.

Everything about Christine was exciting. Being with her was like a game. My fifteen-year-old morality didn't have a chance.

Once a week or so, my bonus from Christine was when she drove us to a motel. She taught me enough tricks to last a lifetime. I could not have been a more willing student.

I had been clueless, a completely blank slate, but so were all men. This was a time when all teenaged boys and many adult men weren't talking about the things Christine was teaching me. The Masters and Johnson sex study Human Sexuality came out in 1966, opening the eyes of the world, but everyman's popular guide, the Joy of Sex didn't come out until 1972. Nothing suggestive was on television. Sex was a big secret cloaked in veils of mystery, hidden behind doors and Pilgrim morality. You could find it in some form in books, but I wasn't that kind of a bookworm, looking for porn for hints to boost my sexual know-how. It would take society a decade to catch up with Christine's lessons and much longer than that to get as open as it is now. She made sure I was well ahead of the game.

She was so beautiful that it was difficult for me to understand why she wasted her time as a cashier.

"Someday, I'll get lucky and get out of the rut," she said. "But in the meantime, the money is good. And these little outings with you are stress relief."

"You never talk about other guys. You do see others, don't you, Christie?"

"Sure, I do, but why should I talk about it? Would you want me to talk about us with someone else?"

I couldn't answer that.

Initially, I kept my relationship with Christine a secret from Patty. However, as intimate partners often do, we eventually shared our hidden truths. Patty confessed to having been involved with my friend Kenji, which led me to reveal my secret about Christine. Our reactions were more of intrigue than anger. I was interested in her relationship with Kenji, and she was intrigued by my relationship with Christine. I shared with her the fact that Christine was seven years older than me, but I didn't emphasize on Christine's striking beauty.

Patty expressed her disgust about my involvement with someone significantly older.

I responded with a laugh and a kiss, telling her to lay back and relax. What followed was intense.

This was the first time Patty had ever screamed.

* * *

Out of the clear blue sky, Christine said we should go out.

"I think in the right clothes, you'll pass for twenty-one," she said.

I dressed in the clothes she had helped me choose.

"We're off to Hollywood, then!"

There was a catch to painting the town red. Christine never paid. I paid for the motel. I knew I would have to pay in Hollywood or wherever we were going.

She was right. At fifteen, I passed for twenty-one at a night club. I'd been thinking that looking twenty-one had nothing to do with it. Back then, the minor thing was not enforced like it is today. Plus, I was with a woman right out of a magazine. Hollywood was wild and wild children were in the clubs with fake ID's or just because no one cared how old they were as long as they had money to pay. I was just another wild child. It was another first for me. We ordered two drinks, but I didn't drink anything with alcohol.

Afterward, we went to a motel that had mirrors above the bed, another first for me. I was high on life and crazy for Christine. I wanted it to go on forever and dreamed that it would. In my defense, it's hard for a fifteen-year-old brain to think with a constant erection.

One day when I arrived at work, the owner and two sales ladies were looking at an advertisement over a display of beer. Christine was smiling proudly behind the counter, listening to them talk about the poster.

Pictured on the display was a young man and woman lying on the beach with a six-pack of a popular beer. Then I realized the young woman was Christine. She looked incredible. Now, in addition to being crazy about her, I was star-struck.

After work that night, we went to a motel.

"You looked fantastic in that poster, Christine!"

"That's the hundredth time you've told me today," she said, laughing.

"You love it," I teased.

"I know," she admitted.

"Now what?"

I scooted closer to get a whiff of that wonderful scent of hers, a turn-on I was growing accustomed to.

I put my hands on her face and kissed her for a very long time, and she never pulled away. I got as hard as a baseball bat.

"I'm going to work as a model," she said. "But we'll talk about that later. First, I'm going to fuck your brains out!"

"Just like that?"

"Just like that."

That was our last night. She didn't quit her job for almost a month, but she didn't give me a chance to take her to bed again. Our Friday nights were a thing of the past.

She finally did leave. Mr. Schultz let me take Christine's job.

"If I see that it interferes with your schoolwork, the deal is off, George. School comes first."

He had said that before. I made it work but taking Christine's job was the first step on the road to my losing interest in school. I hung on to school and work. I had always worked but this was a full-time job.

I assured Mr. Schultz I could handle it, that I could reschedule my classes to work full-time. Instead, I started cutting classes. I was miserable about losing Christine.

My algebra teacher cornered me one morning.

"I wouldn't be as tolerant of your absences if you weren't passing your tests. Any problems, Hatcher?"

"All kinds of family problems," I lied.

* * *

I turned sixteen and bought a car as I had planned. First, I visited Mr. Holmberg at the bank. Being a minor, he couldn't provide a loan without a co-signer. I made a down payment of half the purchase price, and my dad, Leonard, signed a note to the bank for the remaining balance. Across the street from the drugstore, I obtained insurance from an agent. So, I had the car and insurance, but I needed to learn how to drive.

I didn't enroll in the school's driver's education as it wasn't offered until the following year. Instead, my dad taught me how to drive at the East Los Angeles College parking lot in the late afternoons and evenings. It was a huge lot. My practice on other occasions was inconsistent. Learning to drive on the freeway was something I did on my own, but I was quite nervous.

It was easier to drive my Ford than to speed down a steep hill on a bicycle, let go of the handlebars, and maneuver the bike left and right with my knees and balance, as I did every time I descended from Patty's house. Back then, wearing a helmet on a bicycle wasn't common, unless you worked for Red Arrow Messenger.

* * *

I continued to work long hours at the drugstore. As a cashier, I made double what I did as a delivery person or assistant-cashier. I didn't mind the extra work. With Christine gone, the luster of working there was gone, but the better wages kept me giving it my all. A few months after Christine was gone, someone at the store told me to look at the new Playboy magazine that had just come in.

The centerfold "bunny" of the month was Christine.

I took a handful of magazines home, cut out the pictures from one of them, and put them into an album. I didn't put them on my wall where my mother could see them, but when I was alone, I spent hours going through them, closing my eyes, and reliving the times we had together.

* * *

Getting to Patty's house was a breeze. No more bikes. I had my car. It was wonderful. I took Patty, Thelma, and her brother to McDonald's to show off the car. Patty, sitting in the passenger seat, was as excited as I was.

At sixteen, Patty looked killer good.

"Are you still doing sit-ups in the morning before school?"

"You know it. I also do pushups, four sets of fifty at a rapid pace. I sweat up a storm before I get in the shower. I wish we had gym equipment. I could do more."

"I'm doing chin-ups. Check my arms." I flexed.

Patty had a firmer stomach than I did.

"You look fine," I told her every time she undressed. She liked it when I kissed her stomach and breasts. Christine's voice was in my ear to satisfy the woman before turning on the switch to finish. Kids who may have been doing what I did, they knew nothing about foreplay. Christine had made me a master at it. Really.

"No one makes me feel like you do," Patty hugged me tightly. "Thank you."

"No, don't thank me. It sounds horrible."

I continued to see Patty, but it troubled me. I tried to make myself feel better about it. I confessed my feelings to her.

"I feel like I'm using you," I told her. "I come over to see you, and we do it, and I'm gone. It's not right."

"Well, I'll be darned, George Hatcher. You finally reached an adult conclusion."

She laughed at me. I guess we were both insensitive.

"I'm sorry, Patty." I started to leave.

"Aren't we going to do it before you go?"

I turned around and found her smiling at me. She opened her arms.

"Come, George. Use me."

After we did it, I told her, "I treasure what we have between us."

She beamed at me.

"Say that again. It's beautiful. No one has ever said that to me. Or anything to compare."

* * *

My mother gave birth to a baby girl, Mary Martha. When she was very tiny, my mother had me sit down to hold her. It was hard to realize that I was now the middle child. I felt a mix of emotions - excitement to have a new sibling and a sense of responsibility to care for her. Holding Mary Martha, I felt a connection as her older sibling, and I knew that I would always look out for her.

Chapter 6
Twists of Fate

One day, Mom called me at the drugstore, crying hysterically. She had received a letter saying that my older brother Raul, who had gone to Mexico City to the university, was in jail. He had been caught in a stolen car and faced four years of prison. A lawyer in Mexico agreed to take his case for two thousand dollars.

My parents didn't have the money. They had used all their savings to pay the doctor and hospital when my sister Mary was born.

"I don't expect you to worry about this money your brother needs, I'm only letting you know about this tragedy."

"Mom, if I had it I'd give it to you in a split second."

Sniff, "I know that son."

I have always given my mom a portion of the money I earned from my job, both in the past and present. I don't recall the specific reason for doing so, but I do know that she never asked me for it. After my brother went off to the University in Mexico, my mom used to mention that she was sending the money I gave her to support him in his studies there. I never inquired for specifics. For as long as I can remember, my mom has been deeply concerned about my brother, especially after her divorce from my dad.

The money I made with Christine I blew as fast as I made it. After Christine left, I played it straight. I had nothing saved, the down payment on my car had cleaned my savings account out.

I rarely reached out to my father in Douglas, but on this occasion, I decided to give him a call. During our conversation, I shared with him the situation involving my brother. However, his response was far from supportive. He expressed his disapproval by saying, "Your brother's actions are disgraceful, just as your use of another man's name instead of your own is." It was clear that he resented the fact that I went by the name George Hatcher. Whenever he brought up this topic, I would remind him that Leonard had not legally adopted me, and it was too late to revert back to my original name, George Kuri, as everyone already knew me as George Hatcher. Unfortunately, my dad abruptly ended the call by hanging up on me. It was not the first time.

I went to see Thelma and explained my problem.

"I don't have any money saved up," she said. "I can try to borrow a little bit here and there. I'll work on it."

"I truly hate hitting you up for this," I said. "Right now, I can't believe I came and told you about this. I'm sorry."

"It's okay, it's okay. We are like family."

"Thank you, Thelma." I thought about all the gifts she'd given me since I started seeing Patty. She was so nice.

"If I can get the money, I need to know how you will pay it back and how soon."

Out of nowhere, I said, "I'm almost sure I can convince my real dad. I've told you about him. He's in Arizona. Right now, he's upset with my brother for getting in trouble, and he hung up on me when I asked him for help, but I think he'll come around and give me the money to pay it back to you or whoever loans it to me."

Thelma loaned me a thousand of the two thousand I needed. She borrowed from several friends and gave me the money when she received it.

When it looked like Thelma wasn't going to get the second thousand, I pushed even harder. I showed Thelma a neatly typed letter from my dad, his promise in writing that he would send me two thousand to pay off the loan. The only problem was that I had typed the letter, and George Kuri knew nothing of it. It was a lie. I was lying to a friend, Patty's mom.

"Let me keep the letter to show to a couple of my friends and the people I borrowed the first thousand from. They are already asking me when I will pay them back," she said.

"The letter says thirty days," I said. "Give it some extra time, just in case."

Thelma came through with the other thousand. My plan was to start shortchanging the register and giving her partial payments. But without Christine there, I couldn't get myself to do it.

I told my mom I borrowed the money from my boss, the first thousand then the second thousand. She sent the payment to the lawyer in Mexico by Western Union.

A month later, the attorney in Mexico told my mother that he needed fifteen hundred more to make a payoff, or my brother would have to do two years in prison. I went back to Thelma again. She should have shown me the door, but she didn't. I showed her a new letter from my dad that he would send me five thousand in thirty days. He was waiting for a deal to close. This letter was as genuine as the last one, that is to say, not worth the paper it was typed on.

"Thelma, get me the fifteen hundred, and I'll give you the five thousand he sends me. That should help. You can keep the extra for yourself."

Thelma did not say she would not accept the extra fifteen hundred.

I felt horror at what I was doing to this woman who had always been so good to me. I wasn't planning on stealing this money. I had every intention of paying it back but knew from the get-go that it wouldn't be with a five thousand windfall from my dad in Arizona. I did not tell her that the payback would have to be in small payments.

I couldn't stand to see my mother cry about my brother being locked up in a Mexican jail. It was a case of my mother's tears versus Thelma's. My mom won.

Thelma knocked on her people's doors, came up with the fifteen hundred, and gave it to me. I gave it to my mother. She sent it to the Mexican lawyer who ripped us off. Even with the cash, my brother still got two years in prison. I figured the fucking lawyer put one over on us just as I had put one over on Thelma. If it had been my money, I would have gotten over it fast, but owing Thelma three thousand five hundred dollars was mind-boggling for me. It was impossible. It might as well have been a million. In 1958, the minimum wage was a dollar an hour. That's eighty-eight weeks of work. Probably close to two years if you figure in for taxes.

I broke the news to Thelma that the lawyer had cheated us, and that my dad had not come through with the money. She was not happy. Every time I went to see Patty, I'd give Thelma something, ten dollars, twenty, one time, fifty dollars. The nickels and dimes I was giving Thelma were driving her crazy.

"Don't give me any more payments like this," she said. "I need it all at once. Save the money and give it to me in one lump sum. Every time you give me a dime on account, I end up spending it. You've given me two hundred so far.

I need the rest. Just like you borrowed it from me, go borrow it from someone else."

I don't think Thelma ever thought the letters I had shown her were fake. She kept pressing me for the money.

Patty took me aside.

"George, my mom is stressed out like you wouldn't believe. She has to pay that money back," she said. "Get her the money. She helped you when you needed it. You help her out now."

Things got worse. Thelma was a punch press operator. After she got injured at work, no paychecks were coming in. What she got from disability was a fraction of what she made at work.

Stealing like before was the answer but I didn't do it. I felt paranoid. I missed Christine. We always had each other's back.

I felt horrible.

Patty called me late at night to talk about it.

"You haven't been over in three days. I don't see you in school. What gives?"

"I'm fucking embarrassed to see your mom. I'm embarrassed to see you too."

"Being embarrassed with my mom is one thing, but never be embarrassed on my account. You should know that. Get in your Ford and drive over here. My mom is asleep, and so is Steve. Hurry, I need you."

George Hatcher

* * *

I tried hard to avoid Thelma, but it was not always possible. After she hurt her hand and was placed on disability, she told me, "I found a nice apartment on Winter Street. Get someone to buy my house, a thousand to me, and take over the mortgage. It will be in foreclosure by next month."

Thelma should have said, get the thousand and give it to me on the thirty-five hundred you owe me. She didn't say that.

I wasn't even sure what foreclosure meant, but it didn't sound good.

"My dad Leonard can borrow a thousand from a finance company he does business with."

"I'm going to lose the house. I owe ten thousand dollars on it."

I liked her house very much, and it seemed to me to be worth more than eleven thousand dollars. It was on a hillside and had a basement that could easily be remodeled into a small apartment, something I was sure Leonard could take on as a personal project. He was handy. The only thing he hated to do was plumbing.

Thelma stopped pushing for the money I owed her, and instead, pushed me to get my parents to buy the house. I stopped avoiding her.

"I don't want you to feel cheated," I said to her. "It's bad enough I owe you the damn money that went to that crook lawyer."

"If your parents give me a thousand dollars, I will be happy. If I put it up for sale, I have to pay a broker fee. If I get a thousand dollars clear, we move out satisfied." The thousand reminded me of how much my mom had gotten from the sale of the house in Douglas when we left there and came to Los Angeles.

"I wish it was someone else and not my parents," I said.

"I don't care who gets the house. I'm going to lose the house. The bank will become the owner and I get nothing."

My parents were interested. They'd never had the opportunity to own a house of their own. They were excited about it. My banker friend, Mr. Holmberg, was enthusiastic about my parents' excellent credit. I filled out the mortgage application on behalf of my parents, and an appraisal was completed. The appraisal didn't put a dollar amount on value except that a loan of $10,000 on the property left sufficient equity over and above that amount.

A month and a half later, we moved in.

Mr. Holmberg's bank did a mortgage loan for the ten thousand dollars. My parents borrowed a thousand dollars from Allied Finance, a company my dad Leonard had borrowed small sums from. Even with taxes and insurance, the payments were little more than they were paying for rent. It was a good deal. Thelma seemed happy about the thousand she got from my parents. My nerves were frayed when she was going to meet my parents, but when it happened, she didn't mention the money I owed her. My mom would have been terrified if she had learned I had borrowed the money for my brother's lawyer from Thelma and not my boss at the drugstore.

I did come over to check out her new apartment. I mean, it wasn't new, but it was new to them. It was a three-bedroom duplex with the same old furniture in it. It was much smaller, but it was compact and Patty, her mom and brother liked it or said they did.

"I feel bad living in your house," I told Patty.

"Why? I told you, I like this apartment. The house was too big for us, and Mom always complained about the payments every month. Here we pay electric but not water or gas. Rent here is cheap."

"You're okay, Patty. Thanks for making me feel better." I felt a rush of affection for her.

Patty ran her fingers through her straight dark hair, licked her lips, and gave me a familiar come-hither look. She flashed me that smile of hers.

"You aren't leaving without me showing you the bedroom, are you?"

"What about your boyfriend?"

"What about him?" She shrugged.

She took my hand and led the way. It was her same desk and two chairs, same curtain on a different window, same fabulous colorful spread on her little twin bed. The view from her window was nothing to shout about, but I wasn't there to look out the window, anyway. My shoes and jeans landed on the floor. My shirt was on.

"I like how you do me," she said. "You do it differently. There's something about the way you do it, the way you kiss me. When you go down on me, I could die with pleasure."

The smile again.

"I feel so bad about the money I owe your mom. I'm not sure my thing is going to get hard."

"I will take care of it," she said.

"You're so nasty," I said.

"You're blushing, George Hatcher."

Patty rode me with her skirt and underpants still on. I got hard and tossed her panties aside. She reached under her skirt and grabbed me there.

"Relax, big boy, let me drive."

Where did the innocence rush off to?

* * *

It was a good-sized house. My old furniture filled Patty's old bedroom, now my new bedroom. Now I had a view of the balcony and the hills. Mary had Patty's brother's room all painted pink. Leonard had the house painted inside and out, put in new screens and carpet, and redid the hardwood floors. Much later, he remodeled the basement into a bedroom with a kitchen and bathroom. Leonard was a great handyman, but he hired out what he needed to and didn't do the dirty work. The upgrades took money and years. Money was tight. It was always tight. I wished Christine had still been there so we could cover each other's back. But she wasn't there, and I did okay with my weekly paycheck.

My mother stopped working when Mary was born. Leonard's pay was good, but it couldn't handle everything. I contributed money each week as before. I stretched my earnings as best I could. I kept wondering how I could swipe three thousand five hundred dollars to pay Thelma off. All I could come up with was robbing a bank or liquor store, but that was not going to happen. Until I met Christine and partnered up with her, I had never stolen anything before, not ever.

Chapter 7
About Selena

I found it increasingly difficult to focus on school, often contemplating skipping it altogether. Taking tests on Fridays felt like an overwhelming task at times. My main interests lay elsewhere—I was drawn to making money, meeting girls while driving or at the drugstore, and finding opportunities to spend time with Patty whenever her boyfriend was absent. Additionally, I cherished the moments spent at home with my baby sister.

As I headed off to work, I spotted these two girls walking down Whittier Boulevard. One of them totally stood out to me. She had this air of confidence and style, moving with a poise that just seemed beyond her age. Rocking a chic skirt and blouse combo, she owned the sidewalk with her killer fashion sense. Her sandy brown hair cascading down her shoulders framed her face beautifully, enhancing her fair skin. Even though she was all covered up, her beauty and grace shone through. She was a total stunner, oozing charm that was impossible to resist.

As I cruised next to them, the crazy traffic on Whittier Boulevard kind of just blurred out. I couldn't take my eyes off her. She had this classy, composed vibe that said a lot about who she was inside. It was like bam! Love at first sight hit me, and I just had to get them to notice me. But hey, the dream girl and her buddy didn't even glance back in my direction.

Later, as I stood behind the register at the drugstore, the chaos of children buying candy and ice cream surrounded me. Amidst the frenzy of small change and little ones paying in nickels and pennies, I caught a glimpse of the two girls passing by the store. Our eyes met, and for a fleeting moment, I felt a connection. I waved, hoping for a friendly response, but unfortunately, my gesture went unnoticed.

The next day, as I saw them crossing the street toward the drugstore, I politely asked the waiting customers to hold on for just a moment. Stepping out of the front doors, I found myself face to face with them for the first time.

"Buenas Tardes," I greeted them in Spanish, bringing them to a halt. The girl I had come to think of as "Dream Girl" smiled at me. Both of them responded with a friendly "Buenas Tardes."

I switched to English. "Do you believe in love at first sight?" My gaze was fixed on "Dream Girl." Her friend chuckled, but Selena seemed lost in thought, as if weighing her response.

I introduced myself, refraining from handshakes. "Dream Girl" was named Selena, and her friend was Concha.

The growing line at the front register demanded my attention. I asked Selena for her phone number and address. "I believe in love at first sight," she said as she wrote on a 3-ring binder paper.

"Me too," I replied, my eyes locked on her.

Back inside the drugstore, the line quickly dissipated, and my absence went unquestioned by my coworkers. I was in high spirits, with Selena's contact information safely tucked in my shirt pocket.

"Something good must have happened to you today," Louise remarked from her station in cosmetics. Behind her, a colorful array of perfumes filled the shelves, while in front of her, an assortment of make-up products, powders, mirrors, and brushes adorned the counters.

An idea sparked in my mind. "Louise, could you do me a favor and assemble a variety of cosmetics—lipsticks, and all those essentials? I need to send a gift to someone."

"For your mother?" she inquired.

"Not for Mama," I replied.

Louise raised her eyebrows, formed her mouth into an 'o' shape, and nodded conspiratorially.

"I'm guessing she could be around nineteen or twenty."

"She's older than you," Louise teased. Although talkative, I found her company enjoyable.

Louise selected an assortment of purple-hued items, placed them in a clear cellophane bag, and tied it with a purple bow. It looked elegant, akin to something my mother would have crafted in her florist shop.

"Nice purple bow," I said. "You should do this for a living."

Louise thumped me on the shoulder, laughing. "You're such a guy," she said. "That's lavender."

"You're the best."

The delivery boy, Lance, was a skinny kid from Hollenbeck Junior High. I promised him I'd give him a dollar if he got back from the delivery by five. He lit out like his seat was on fire, and lava was after him.

When Louise called me to the phone, I knew it had to be Selena even before hearing her voice. Lance wasn't back yet. She spoke in English. I loved her accent.

"I hope I didn't get you in trouble calling at work, but those things you sent me by messenger...I really don't know what to say."

"Don't say a thing. It's my pleasure. If there's anything you want to exchange, bring it over, or I'll send the messenger back."

"I'm not used to anyone being this nice to me," she said. "We don't even know each other."

"We can fix that fast," I said in Spanish.

"Your Spanish is perfect!"

"It was my first language," I said.

Our conversation continued in Spanish.

"Go back to work. Call me when you can talk. I love everything you sent. Thank you very much."

Lance made it back before five, and I gave him four quarters. He was thrilled for about three minutes until Louise gave him three orders to deliver. He lit out like he was being chased by the football team from Hollenbeck Junior High. They hadn't won a game in ten years.

Three nice phone booths are in the back corner of the drugstore. With the door shut, you can have a private conversation. An hour later, I commandeered a booth, dropped in my coin, and called her.

"It's me," I said.

"Sentí escalofríos cuando escuché tu voz."

"I got chills when I heard your voice right now," she said in Spanish.

"Is that good or bad? I mean, chills could be because I frightened you, or you left the window open."

She laughed.

I loved her laugh. It was like music.

"This kind of chill is good," she said.

"Want to get a shake or something to eat?"

"How about tomorrow morning?" she countered.

"Deal. Are you in school?" I asked.

"Roosevelt, same as you."

"I've never seen you there before."

"I've seen you there several times. I only take an English class. I graduated from school in Mexico. Roosevelt offers an adult English class during the day."

"I didn't know that."

"It's a three-hour class and I need it. My English is terrible."

"Talk to me in English and I'll tell you if it's terrible."

"Okay," she replied.

Our conversation continued in Spanish.

"How old are you?" I asked.

"I'm twenty. How about you?"

"I'm sixteen, going on thirty," I said.

Selena laughed again.

"Bye, George," she said in a whisper that sent me dancing back to the register.

The next morning, I picked up Selena and Concha, with Concha sitting in the back seat. Throughout the ride, Selena's delightful presence and the exquisite fragrance that lingered around her lent an enchanting air to the car. As I dropped Concha off at school, and she departed with three words: "bye for now."

Driving away, I asked, "Would you like to see Santa Monica Beach?"

"Wherever you wish to take me," she said. She slid close to me. I wanted to pat her thigh in approval but I didn't do it.

"What part of Mexico are you from?" I inquired, and we mostly conversed in Spanish during the journey.

"Juarez."

"So, are you going to stay in LA, or are you here temporarily?"

"I'm not sure."

It was a cloudy gray day, as we headed toward Santa Monica Beach and just as cloudy when we got there.

"Curious about why I'm here in Los Angeles?" This was just one of the inquiries I hadn't voiced. I took a moment to admire her beautiful features.

"Absolutely."

"I used to date a guy in Juarez, Sergio was his name. One evening, I didn't return home and that marked the start of my fallout with my parents."

"So, you're saying you stayed over at Sergio's."

"Correct, it's not like we hadn't been intimate before, but the real transgression was not coming home that night. My parents were livid. They claimed that if their friends discovered this, it would tarnish their reputation and that my actions were setting a bad example for my nine younger sisters."

"Are they all as stunning as you?"

"Me not beautiful. My sisters are beautiful."

"Selena you are beautiful."

Selena was a chatterbox. I was thankful that she felt comfortable enough to share her story with me.

"My aunt, where I live now, is a mother to six children. She's a divorcee and relies on the financial support my father provides for my upkeep. His directives to her are clear - enforce strict discipline - and she does. I couldn't step out last night when you asked me because she probably say no go out. If she discovered I was here with you, she'd likely alert my father and that would not be good for me."

"You're 20. You're not a child. At least not here."

"In Mexico I'm an adult at age 18, just like here. Doesn't work that way if you live at home like I was and still depending on my father for support. Living with my aunt is same as living at home in Juarez."

The beach was overcast, but we didn't mind. We took off our shoes and walked on the sand. There were sea birds, and salt spray in the air, and seaweed on the ground, and the waves washed over our toes up to our ankles and then subsided, sinking our feet in the sand. We sat down on the warm dune and spent the morning watching the ocean. We weren't alone, but it felt like we were. An old guy with a metal detector carried a sack of his junk finds. Other people were collecting shells and just walking around. No one paid attention to us, which was perfect. Around noon, we ate at a seafood restaurant.

Once we had gotten off the subject of her parents, the conversation was jolly. She had a wonderful sense of humor. I laughed so much in those hours we were together that I felt reborn.

"We talked about everything except sex," she said soberly. "What do you think about sex?"

I may have blushed. "I love sex."

"You're only sixteen," she said with a smile. "Tell me."

We laughed.

"Tell you what?" I was playing her.

She took my hand and playfully pulled it, like a come on, tell me.

"I got an early start," I said. "Let me tell you when we meet again."

"Promise?"

"Absolutely, I promise."

I wanted to ask if she'd tell me about her sex experiences but I didn't do that.

Before getting out of the car a block from her aunt's house she said, "Sixteen. You're so so young." She said this in Spanish.

"It goes fast," I said. "In October, I'll be seventeen, then…"

She laughed.

* * *

As I drove to work, thoughts of Patty and myself consumed my mind. Despite knowing that Patty had multiple boyfriends, and that they were likely intimate with her, I couldn't change the situation. Similarly, Patty couldn't control my wild nature. We were best friends, but exclusivity was not part of our dynamic. My previous relationship with Christine had been imbalanced, with her holding all the power over me. With Selena, I yearned for a lasting connection, not just a fleeting encounter that would catch me off guard. Most of my dates with girls my age were devoid of physical intimacy, some fondling and kissing, unlike my experiences with Patty or Christine.

I was in no hurry to have sex with Selena. I barely knew her.

I loved her.

* * *

In the afternoon on a break, I called Selena.

"Want me to ask your aunt if she'll let you go out tonight?"

"What if she says no?"

"We'll never know unless we ask."

Her aunt wasn't so bad. I paid special attention to my clothes and my manners. When I was there, I listened to her and responded politely. I won't say she grilled me, but she did have a lot of questions. I must have come up with the right answers. I know she looked at my car, it was a nice car for a person my age. "Is that your car?" Her aunt asked.

"Yes, it's mine," I said. "Half of it belongs to the bank because I make payments."

Her aunt laughed. Selena laughed too, watching how I handled her aunt.

Her aunt agreed we could go out that night on a date.

Selena and I spent the night driving around Hollywood. She had never been there before and was fascinated by the lights and the hippies walking on the boulevard. We had a hamburger and spent hours talking. We talked about our childhoods and told each other funny stories about our lives. She told me about her sisters and how close she felt to her youngest sister, Luna.

"She's wild. She tells dirty jokes non stop."

"Dirty jokes, wow."

"She's so funny. I miss her."

"I bet you do. I'd miss my little sister if I went to another country, and she's just a baby."

"I miss all my sisters."

I saw her eyes glisten and took her hand. Suddenly, she said, "you promised to tell me about your sex experiences, or experience. What have you done?"

"It's raw," I said. "Are you sure you want to hear?"

Selena smiled. "Tell me, tell me."

I didn't start with Patty, I started by telling her about Christine. Every once in a while she'd say, "My my." In Spanish it sounds better.

At some point we kissed. It was a long kiss. A very wet kiss.

"You set me on fire," she spoke in my lips. "So much you done in short life you are sixteen."

On another date I told her about Patty, even told her about the money I owed Patty's mom, Thelma.

"Poor lady must be very mad at you, borrowing from her friends then not having the money to pay them back."

"I should force her to take small payments like I had started. But she won't take the payments."

"It's not only that, you admit you lied to her that your father Kuri was going to give you the money to pay the loans back."

It was like Selena was scolding me, I suppose it was the four years older that she had on me. I almost took it personal but I didn't. Selena was right. Not even Patty pushed it on me as hard as Selena did. Not sure why I told Selena all the details when all she was wanting to hear was the sex experiences. It was like I needed to confess. Needed it off my chest.

* * *

My daily routine underwent a change. Every morning, I would pick up Selena and Concha, drop Concha off at school, and then drive with Selena to the beach. We loved the ocean. I drove to Redondo Beach, Huntington Beach, Plays del Rey, Malibu, and others.

We made it a point to be in school on Fridays. Especially when they had tests. However, Selena didn't seem to care much about attending school. She only went because her aunt expected her to and because she said it helped her English get better.

If I were in Selena's shoes, I would have left her aunt's house, found a job, and become independent from her parents. But I never brought up this idea. Perhaps she didn't want to work, but I couldn't understand why she would choose to live in a cramped apartment with all those kids who belonged to her aunt, feeling trapped by her father who was all the way in Juarez, Mexico.

I also never asked her if she was in touch with Sergio, the boyfriend she admitted having a long relationship with and with whom she had spent the night that caused the problem with her parents. I didn't want to know.

In the afternoon, I took her home and then went to work. At night, I picked her up again, and we would take a drive or go to a movie. I usually showed up with something for her aunt: perfume, make-up, a flower, a candy bar.

"I don't think you have to give my aunt any more gifts," she told me. "She's sold on you. We're safe."

I got used to and expected the kisses and the reassurance as we drove. Selena was the most touchy-feely person I had ever met. She was open and affectionate, using her hands and lips on my skin, and giving hugs at every opportunity.

"I feel a sense of peace around you," she said while tugging at my curly hair.

"Ditto."

"What's ditto?"

"It's like saying 'me too.'"

Out of nowhere, she flung her arms around me and showered me with kisses. Although I wished to believe that her displays of affection were solely for me, there were moments when I couldn't shake the thought of Sergio, her boyfriend, crossing her mind during these spontaneous acts of love and affection.

We were in the car, eating a pastrami. It was served in halves. Good thing. It was huge. We divided it. Between bites, I pushed her to use as little Spanish as possible.

"I'm jealous," she said in English before switching to Spanish. "You and Christine went to night clubs, why can't you and I do it?"

I thought about it. Neither of us looked like high school students. I had clothes that I had purchased with

Christine's assistance for going out, and Selena was always dressed fashionable and nicely."We can do that," I said.

In the real world, Selena was just a few months from her twenty-first birthday. I had a bunch of years to go before I reached that age. We managed to enter the club successfully. The door staff's scrutiny was minimal, but when we tried to order alcohol, the scrutiny heightened. Our successful infiltration of the club opened up new opportunities for us to explore other venues. These venues always demanded hefty entry fees. This was money I could have offered to Thelma, had she been open to accepting partial payments, or if I had exercised enough discipline to save it until I had a substantial amount to give her. The cover charges increased the overall expense. Day and night, I was plagued by guilt over the money I owed Patty's mom. I should have exerted more effort to find a solution.

On another night we were in a vibrant nightclub in the heart of Hollywood. The pulsating music filled the air, creating an energetic atmosphere that resonated with the rhythm of the night. The dance floor was alive with couples swaying and moving to the beat, their bodies gracefully intertwining in a mesmerizing display of passion and freedom. The lights were dimmed, casting a soft glow over the room, while flickering candles adorned the tables, adding a touch of intimacy to the ambiance. It was a scene straight out of a movie, where time seemed to stand still and every moment held the promise of excitement and adventure. We were both drinking virgin Margaritas.

Selena spoke to me in Spanish. "No me has insinuado nada, ¿Acaso no te atraigo?" (You haven't made a move on me. Don't I attract you?) We were at a club in Hollywood, where the music was loud. "Is it because I went all the way with Sergio?" Sitting closely, our bodies were just inches apart, facing each other.

"I don't care what you did with Sergio," I replied. "I want you more than you can imagine." I took her hand and placed it there. "Do you believe me?"

It was dark, and no one could see or was bothering to look for hands under the table. Selena smiled, then squeezed, just hard enough. "I want to," she said. "Estoy tan caliente que no awanto."

On our way to her aunt's house we passed the drugstore. It was after ten so it was closed. I pulled into the parking lot in the back that was not illuminated and we were totally alone. Just as it should be. "We can wait and go to a hotel when we're not running late or we can do it here and now," I said.

"Now," she whispered. Our bodies fused in the back seat of my car, our kisses turning passionate in an instant. The passing of time appeared to cease as we gave in to the seductive heat of our desires.

After that night, we practically stopped going to nightclubs and instead we'd go to a motel. The distance between the drugstore and the motel was roughly one mile. Identification was not required; all I needed was cash. The only inquiry made was regarding the duration of our desired room rental. It was the ideal configuration. We were able to park in front of our own door with privacy because the motel's parking area was hidden from view from the Boulevard.

"Is this where you and Christine came? It's okay if it is."

"No, that was another motel. Not far away."

"I'm sorry, I shouldn't have asked that."

I chuckled. "You can ask me anything."

Back in 1959, the motel offered rooms at the price of $3 for the night or $2 for 8 hours. The bedding was clean, a detail that both Selena and I found crucial. The room was modest, featuring nothing more than a bed and a small bathroom with a tub and shower and a television. There were no additional amenities such as a coffee pot. The simplicity of the space was exactly what we wanted.

In addition, there was a small wrapped bar of soap provided for use at the washbasin and in the shower if we chose to freshen up. After the first visit I brought a toiletry bag from the drugstore with everything we both needed.

An unexpected reaction from Selena occurred during an intimate moment with me. She twisted her body and crossed her legs while yelling that I couldn't do that. Eventually she gave in and allowed it to take place.

After, she remarked, "It's a first for me." Her entire body was shaking, and she appeared extremely shaken. She had climaxed.

"Are you okay?"

She responded by pulling my hair and guiding my head back down to its original position.

* * *

My seventeenth birthday was celebrated on a bed at the motel. Selena told her aunt she was spending the night with Concha. I told my parents I was going with friends to the mountains.

"Know what I have for your birthday?" Selena asked.

"I have a pretty good idea," I said.

We were naked under the covers, and I reached for her beautiful breasts. Passion, sex, fascination, love, infatuation-who knows what is what at seventeen?

She giggled and pulled away.

"Wait. It's your turn today. I've been taking advantage of you."

It took me a moment to catch on. Selena helped my thought process by sliding toward the foot of the bed. I caught her by the hand.

"You don't have to."

"Yes, I do," she said on her way down. "I fantasize about this. If you get any bigger as you grow up, all your girlfriends, me included may have a problem.

She said girlfriends like it was a free for all. Her words invaded the space we were in.

Selena gave me a couple of kisses that weren't on my lips.

She pulled away a little bit. "You're only seventeen and look at this."

* * *

The words, "I love you," comes easy when you are wrapped up in each other. A number of times I uttered those words to her and each time, she would pause a moment to say. "You don't need to love me for us to do what we do."

It bothered me when she said this. I didn't let it show.

After a little time, sex was not just at the motel. Everything we did together was colored in laughter and fun. Sometimes, we'd grab a quickie in the back seat of my car in a busy parking lot, or in the snow while skiers whizzed past. We were young explorers caught up in each other. I never did that with Patty or Christine. I had gone pretty far with a number of girls, but never as publicly as with Selena. I got a thrill out of it, but it was Selena that opened the door to this new adventure of having daring sex. "You're an exhibitionist," I'd say to her.

"Takes one to know one," she'd say with a scream of laughter.

We would push our limits, do something daring, and then spend hours talking about what we'd just done. We laughed uncontrollably over how we screwed at the movies in a janitor supply room without getting caught. Every moment together was exciting and fun. In the beginning, I had thought Selena was shy, but the truth was that she was fearless in the face of unusual experiences, and that meant anything out of the ordinary.

"Did you do stuff like this with Sergio? You don't have to tell me."

She frowned.

"No."

"I don't know why I asked," I said. "I'm sorry."

The frown disappeared.

"Ask me anything you want when you want," she said.

She got that line from me.

* * *

The motel became like a clubhouse for Selena and me, providing the privacy we needed to talk, watch television, and be together. At my age, it was difficult to find a place where we could do these things. With Patty, we had her room and a mom who respected our privacy. It was unlikely that we'd find that kind of freedom anywhere else.

The motel was our go-to place. I'd often bring take-out food, and we'd have our meals there. Over time, I became familiar to the managers, and as a regular visitor, I managed to negotiate better prices. Selena never had to go to the office with me when I checked in.

One day I said, "This is a conversation, I'm not proposing. I want to know if you'd marry me?"

"She propped herself up on her elbow and looked down at me.

"But why, George? We're happy, aren't we?"

"Of course. It's because we're so happy that I don't want to ever lose you."

She sighed. I never heard her sigh like that before. "No strings George. Come on, don't spoil it."

"Spoil it?"

She kissed me.

Another time. "You said you weren't sure if you loved Sergio."

"Right now, I only think of us, not him. We spend more time together than most married people. We have our whole lives ahead of us. We don't need marriage."

No matter what, she was my senior by almost four years and once in a while she mothered me into silence. "I've given you all of me," she said.

She was right. She'd given me her body but I wanted more.

"You weren't the first person I went to bed with. You have to be sure you love me enough to overlook that and not throw it in my face someday."

"I can't believe you just said that." I said sternly.

It wasn't lost on me how happy Selena was when I stopped talking about marriage. When I dropped the marriage talk, she stopped talking about becoming a pariah in Mexico because of her one night out with Sergio. I laid off the sensitive topics, and then everything else between us was light and fun and laughs.

I'd dropped Selena off at Concha's house, snuck home, and hadn't even gotten in bed yet. Tomorrow was Monday, a school day, and I was planning how to squeeze in some sleep, get to work, and have time with Selena.

The phone rang. I grabbed it because no one called my parents so late. It had to be Selena.

It was Patty. "I'm so sorry to call so late. If it had been your mom or dad, I would have hung up. It's just I've been trying to reach you three nights in a row. I don't see you in school. Kenji says you are still ditching. Are you okay?"

"Aw, Patty. Thanks for checking on me. I love you all the more for that."

"Love me? You never told me that before."

"Well, I should have told you that a long time ago. I mean we are in love like best friends, not like Romeo and Juliet. Do I make sense?"

"I understand," she said. "Now, tell me what's going on."

"Who are you seeing currently?" I asked.

"Why?"

"I'll come over tomorrow night if you don't have anyone there."

"Deal. Come over. You need to tell mom something about the money."

"I wish she had not stopped me from giving her the small payments. By now, I wouldn't owe her so much."

"You know she spends the money. The people she borrowed from want a lump sum back, same as how they gave it to her."

"See you tomorrow," she said. "Stop ditching. If you need help with homework, bring it over."

"We need to talk," I said.

"We do. I'll be waiting. We could have lunch together at school. Want to?"

"I won't be in school tomorrow," I admitted.

* * *

The result of last night's phone call was that all day Monday, I worked and worried a little about running into Thelma, but I looked forward to seeing Patty, even if she was going to be sure to nag me about ditching school. As an emergency gift, I got a package of fancy bath powder and took it with me when I drove to their place in my car. Winter street is big and wide, and with so many apartments competing for spots, parking is terrible. I found a spot around the corner. My books, notebooks, and everything were in my schoolbag in the trunk, so I grabbed it and carried it with me back around the corner, through the little front yard, into the little back yard of the duplex. The door to Patty's was really her window. Patty saw me standing there, and I didn't have to knock. Like her other boyfriends, I climbed in through her open window and into a big hug.

"I've been so worried about you!" Patty said. "I got all the homework assignments from school. I hope you don't mind. I went to your teachers and got it."

Her books were stacked on her little desk, and she made room by moving stuff to the bed. She gave me a pile of folders from my teachers. It was almost like it used to be, except we weren't on the balcony in the house I was now living in, and we didn't really share the classes anymore.

"Thanks for talking to my teachers," I told her. I gave her the bath powder and told her she could have it, or she could give it to Thelma for me, or she could just stick it in the bathroom and not say anything. We set to work shoulder-to-shoulder, and it lit a little fire under me, and I suddenly wanted to catch up with school.

I did as much as I could. It wasn't dark yet, so there was time, and nothing was that hard to figure out. After we'd had enough of books and schoolwork, we put our stuff away.

"Who are you seeing?" I asked.

Patty said she was seeing a guy named Jessie. Said I didn't know him. He was in one of her classes. As the conversation progressed, Patty curiously probed into my love life, to which I responded with the name, Selena. With a sense of finality, I said, "I intend to make her my wife." Patty, with her eyes directed towards the ceiling, shook her head in disbelief. "Already planning on tying the knot? Goodness, have you lost your senses in the short span since we last met?"

"I'm a nut case for sure," I laughed.

She agreed with a laugh of her own, "Have you had sex with her?"

"A lot of sex."

"Is the sex so good you want to marry her?"

"That's not why I want to marry her. —I love her."

Patty, look at me." My face was 10 inches from hers. "I love her."

As we sat on her bed, both cross-legged and fully dressed, a prolonged silence enveloped the room until she finally spoke, saying, "In that case, good luck, my dear friend." Her eyes closed, and when they reopened, they were moist with tears.

* * *

I didn't work on Sunday. Selena and I spent the whole day at the motel, watched TV, fooled around, and ate takeout, tacos and burritos. She drank Pepsi and I liked Coca-Cola chilled in a Styrofoam cooler we brought along.

I knew she didn't want to hear it, but every so often I'd blurt out, "let's get married." I just couldn't help myself. I knew she didn't want to talk about it. Plus, I didn't have money, I owed on my car, and I owed Thelma. How stupid of me to keep pushing for marriage. I was just a seventeen-year-old, thinking I had all the brains, experience, wisdom, and cojones of my years.

* * *

One morning in Santa Monica, I said, "Someday, I'm going to buy a house on the beach."

"I believe you," she replied. "You're smart. When I listen to you talk, I think you can do anything you want to do. I wish you were not missing so much school."

"You're missing school, too," I retorted.

She stuck her tongue out at me. "Only English lessons, and I get my English from you now. I feel guilty about you not being in school."

I kissed her. "I went part of Monday and part of Friday. Don't feel bad about it. It's my choice. You have nothing to do with my ditching."

"Not true, George," she replied.

We strolled hand in hand along the water's edge, heading toward the pier. The sunset adorned the water and sky with a myriad of colors, filling my heart with anticipation. I wished this moment could last forever. If only she would say yes, we could be perfect together for eternity. We were both too young to marry, but I held onto the belief that we would find a way. I had no established profession and doubted I would graduate from school. Where would I work? How long could I sustain a job at the drugstore? My thoughts kept returning to the boyfriend she had left in Mexico, the one she wasn't certain she still loved. If she married me, that boy would be completely out of the picture. Marriage seemed like the perfect solution.

A week went by, a succession of perfect days with Selena. How were the days perfect when I was constantly trying to convince her to marry me, and I didn't have a pot to piss in? I was a seventeen-year-old high school kid living with my parents. I didn't have a home for a wife. I gave my parents money from my paycheck. But *looking back* I still spent so much time trying to convince Selena that we had to get married. *Looking back*, I shake my head in wonderment. I was a total dummy.

* * *

One evening I was at work. Selena's aunt walked into the drugstore. I was slammed with customers. She motioned that she would wait and remained standing where I could see her. I checked as fast as I could, but I had a sense of dread due to her expression. The first thing that popped into my mind was that Selena was pregnant, and her aunt was there to read the riot act. But if that had been the circumstance, surely it would have been Selena to say something to me.

My assistant took over the register. Selena's aunt's hesitant manner worried me.

"Is something the matter?" I asked.

She held out a letter.

"Selena told me to give you this."

Before I could say or do anything, she was out the door. I looked down at the envelope, and even before I read a word, a chill went through my body. Something was wrong. I needed privacy, so I went into the restroom before opening the envelope. Selena's neat handwriting stared at me.

> Mi querido amor,
> Para cuando leas esto, estaré en un avión rumbo a casa. Me resulta difícil escribir esto, pero contigo debo ser honesta. En este momento, no puedo comprometerme a casarme contigo.
> Hay dos razones detrás de mi decisión. En primer

lugar, debo reconciliarme con mis padres. Ni siquiera llaman a mi tía para preguntar por mí. Esto no puede continuar. Necesito enfrentarlos y resolver la distancia que ha crecido entre nosotros. No puedo permitir que un solo error cree una barrera duradera entre mis padres y yo.

La segunda razón tiene que ver con Sergio. Necesito entender mis sentimientos hacia él. Debo ver a Sergio nuevamente para saber realmente dónde está mi corazón. ¿Cómo puedo considerar la idea de casarme contigo sin esta respuesta vital? Te aprecio demasiado como para contemplar un futuro ensombrecido por las incertidumbres. No puedo arriesgarme a romper tu corazón. Sería injusto pedirte que esperes, así que no lo haré. Sin embargo, en mi egoísmo, espero que lo hagas. En el fondo, siento que volveré a ti, pero no puedo hacer un compromiso hasta que mi vida esté en orden y tenga claridad dentro de mí misma.

Si nunca tengo la fortuna de verte de nuevo, quiero que sepas que el tiempo que pasamos juntos ha sido el más feliz de mi vida. El recuerdo de nuestros momentos calentará mi corazón eternamente. Por favor, no albergues resentimiento hacia mí.

Tuya,
Selena

My dearest love,

By the time you read this, I'll be on a plane heading home. It's difficult for me to write this, but with you, I must be honest. I cannot, at this time, commit to marrying you.

There are two reasons behind my decision. Firstly, I must reconcile with my parents. They don't even call my aunt anymore to check up on me. This can't go on. I need to face them and resolve the distance that has grown between us. I cannot have a single mistake create a lasting barrier between my parents and me.

The second reason concerns Sergio. I need to understand my feelings for him. I must see Sergio again to truly know where my heart lies. How can I entertain the idea of marrying you without this vital answer? I cherish you too deeply to contemplate a future overshadowed by uncertainties. I cannot risk breaking your heart. It would be unfair to ask you to wait, so I won't. Yet, in my selfishness, I hope that you do. Deep down, I feel that I will return to you, but I cannot make a commitment until my life is in order and I have clarity within myself.

If I never have the fortune of seeing you again, I want you to know that the time we spent together has been the happiest of my life. The memory of our moments will warm my heart eternally. Please, do not harbor resentment toward me.

Yours,

Selena

I folded the page. I put it in the envelope and the envelope in my shirt pocket. I took off my white smock and walked out of the restroom and drugstore in a daze. It was all very mechanical. I was in shock. I hardly saw the many customers I shouldered through to get to the door. I made it to the car and put the pedal to the floor. My brain was not working at all. My heart was racing, and a big knot of pain settled in the center of my chest. Ten minutes later, I was stopped by the highway patrol.

"I normally arrest anyone crazy enough to do ninety," the officer said. "Can you give me a good reason not to?"

Tears ran down my face. I couldn't answer.

"Are you sober? Are you alright?"

I managed to speak. "Someone in my family just died," I told him. It was almost true.

Chapter 8
I joined the Navy

I stood in the principal's office with the door shut. There was a chair, but I did not feel like sitting. The glass in the top half of his door was opaque, but through it, I could make out the school secretaries, the vice principal, and other people mulling about. They were already part of my past. I would not miss high school.

The school principal shook his head in concern and looked up from my parents' letter, which I'd forged.

"Why quit school, son? Your grades are fairly good, and you should think of the future."

My mind was made up. I'd already cleaned out my locker.

* * *

The ELA recruiting office was a small storefront with a glass door. I had nothing left here in LA. I had made up my mind to find my future behind that door. I saw nothing earth-shattering inside: a wooden desk, brochures, a guy whose head was practically shaved. He was in uniform.

"You want to join the Navy?" the recruiter asked as he scrutinized my paperwork and me. "You're underage. We'll need your parents' consent."

At home, I broke the news to my parents.

"I was bored with school," I lied. "I have a better chance of getting an education if I go into the Navy."

I trusted that the Navy would take me away from the scene of my heartbreak and get me a better education than high school. All the billboards said join the Navy and go to school.

I delivered my parents' signed consent forms to the Navy recruiter. I ran into a problem with my name. I turned to my boss, Mr. Schultz, who referred me to an attorney. I went to seek counsel the same day.

"My real name is George Kuri. My father is still living, but I've been using the name Hatcher since I moved to LA at ten years old. Everyone knows me as Hatcher, but I can't join the Navy as George Hatcher until it's legal."

The attorney said that an adoption would take a long time and would require the consent of my real father. I could easily just change my name. The Navy would accept the consent form signed by a Superior Court Judge and let me enlist as George John Hatcher. Without consent or adoption, I would have to enlist as George Kuri Jr. I didn't want to do that. It cost two hundred dollars to hire the lawyer who handled the change of name petition. I thought it was expensive. That's how much I knew about attorney fees.

* * *

I drove to some places I'd been to with Selena. I relived the memories we'd created together. I did not question whether I was heartbroken or angry. I often cried when I was alone, only to be ashamed afterward. I thought about hating her, but a sweet memory would come along and wipe those negative thoughts away. I loved her.

* * *

Patty let me have it.

"You still want to marry this girl who skipped back to Mexico to find out if she still loves her ex-boyfriend?"

"You asked her to marry you, and it made her run off to Mexico. How can you still want her? What happened to you? Are you the same person that girls in school were dying to date? Are you the same person who won student body vice president by a landslide? Are you the same person who acted in two plays when we were in drama, and the audience clapped like you were Elvis? What happened to you?"

"I lost something along the way. You don't know because you haven't fallen in love."

George Hatcher

We were fully dressed facing each other, barefoot, sitting close enough on her twin bed that I felt her breath on my face when she spoke.

"I should have stuck by you," I said. "I'm sorry if I hurt you."

Patty's scolding frown left her pretty face. She touched me, leaned forward, and kissed a tear rolling down my face.

"You didn't hurt me. You're my best friend. I think about you every single day, and when I'm with another boy, I think of you then too. We are never going to get married, and it's okay. We can stay best friends forever."

We hugged and fell back on the pillow, our lips pressed together.

I left Patty's house that night the way I got in. I did not want to meet up with Thelma. Patty thought it was best. She said her mom was totally pissed at me about the money I owed her.

The Navy was finally satisfied with my paperwork. The document that finalized the deal was the Superior Court order granting the motion to change my name to George John Hatcher. It did not require my real dad's consent, even though I was not eighteen.

I said goodbye to everyone.

* * *

On January 18, 1960, I was sworn into the US Navy. I was seventeen. In October I would turn eighteen.

The other recruits and I were taken to San Diego where we spent nine weeks in boot camp. The tough atmosphere was a total bitch on my body and brain. The grueling training and routine punishments were a distraction from heartbreak, but I didn't welcome it with open arms. The intensity got so bad that I felt like exploding.

On the grounds was a half-scale ship built of concrete where we had drills. The mess hall was big. The food was great and all we could eat, but they never gave us enough time to finish. It was so wasteful. I suppose it was part of the discipline.

The barracks were our living space. Sparse, just bunks with no personal space and shelving that acted as dividers. We were given little space to put our things, and everything had to be exactly in the right location.

You'd think it would be impossible to sleep in a room with so many men, but they kept us moving before dawn till after dark and pushed us to our limits. We collapsed into our bunks and slept like the dead.

I was hardening emotionally. At seventeen, I felt like I was three times older. The constant tension made me angry and mean, and that led to me having three fistfights. If we had been caught, we would have paid for it. Fighting is not something the navy forgives you for.

The whole purpose of basic training is to ready you to jump to your work fast and live in tight quarters on a ship without losing your head.

* * *

My group was punished at target practice and ordered to clear all the loose rocks from a portion of ground and throw them over the cliff, but not at any targets—the targets being Marines working at the bottom of the cliff. We didn't follow orders.

I learned that two Marines had suffered bad cuts. The news shocked me back to earth. It frightened me to learn that I may have been responsible for needlessly hurting another human being.

Up until halfway through boot camp, I wasn't social at all, but then I settled down. I made up with the three sailors I'd fought early on. I made friends with others. Being around friends helped to a degree, but Selena was still on my mind. The longing was constant torture. My friends and I told each other our hard luck stories. I wasn't the only one with a Selena who had gone astray. We all had stories about the one who got away.

A third of the guys joined to see the world, a third for the benefit to their spouse and career, and a third to drown their heartbreak. Payday came. It wasn't a huge amount of money, but there was cash in my pocket - two weeks' worth. I wished it had been a little more, but it was burning a hole in my pocket. Cash inevitably reminded me of Thelma. Part of me knew I should be sending it all to Thelma to pay down the debt. I preferred stealing to borrowing money. Owing Thelma was a nightmare. Today, as I write this, thirty-five hundred dollars is still a lot of money, but back then it was an immense amount of money.

"We got that ten-hour liberty coming up," a friend said, inviting me along. "Want to mess around in San Diego?"

I did get intimate during that day-pass, but it was mechanical. The whole experience was like being with a robot who kept looking at her watch. I thought of Patty and got excited, thought of Christine, and got excited. I tried not to think about Selena and intimacy.

Near the end of training, my unit officer called me into his office.

"Hatcher, you ain't going to graduate with this unit. You've flunked the swim test three times, and you're out of strikes."

He told me I'd be transferring to another unit in the morning. It would put me back three weeks-three extra weeks of hell-three extra weeks before I could take a two-week leave. I had to do something.

Boot camp had taught me that the brass avoided confrontations involving civilians. I figured there had to be an angle. Everything had an angle. Some people called it manipulation. I called it survival.

After dinner, I called Western Union in Los Angeles from the phone center at the base. I billed the call to my mom.

I sent a telegram to the commandant's office saying that the huge engagement reception costing hundreds of dollars had already been planned and paid for, and as it was to be held during my scheduled furlough, it couldn't be canceled on such short notice. The message was allegedly from my mother.

"My son's father is a retired Captain in the US Navy, and he will be horrified when he learns that the Navy failed to teach his son how to swim. I appeal to you to permit my son to undergo these tests again in order to graduate with his unit. I am confident you will understand the position this has placed me in."

Neither my dad nor stepdad were retired Navy. It was all a lie. I remembered the letters I had typed for Thelma to get her to loan me the money I was after.

I signed it 'a concerned Navy mother and wife, Martha Hatcher.'

Before noon the following day, the unit officer sent for me.

"Hatcher, I just got my ass chewed out over you, and I want to tell you I'm not very happy."

"I don't understand, sir," I said, trying to sound as innocent as I could.

"Just listen, Hatcher. I am personally going to take you across the street to the pool, and we are not going to leave until you pass every swim test you flunked!"

"Yes, sir. I'll do my best, sir." I could swim, but I was never a good swimmer.

The tower was taller than any diving board. Looking straight up from the foot of it, it looked freakishly tall until you climbed it. Looking down, it seemed even higher. One of the tests was stepping off that monster tower as though you were stepping off a ship. After hitting the water, you had to take off your shirt, tie it off, and use it as a life jacket while swimming on your back.

I perform best under pressure.

I graduated with my company as scheduled. I even became buddies with the petty officer during that last week. The day I was leaving, I went into his office to say goodbye.

"Hatcher, you rascal, it's been a pleasure," he said. "Tell me the truth. Is your dad a retired captain?"

"My dad was never in the service," I said with a tiny grin.

"You son-of-a-bitch! That telegram was fake?" He took a cigar, bit the end off, and spat. "I had a feeling it was a crock of shit!"

He extended his hand for me to shake anyway. Then we both started laughing.

"You know, kid," he said, "I'm going to miss you."

Chapter 9
Selena Returns

Nine weeks in boot camp had left me trim and solid. On the first day of my furlough, I had my uniforms tailored. My waist had dropped from 33" to 29". The next day, I took the bus to LA to see my parents. My dad picked me up at the Greyhound station, and we went home to a huge breakfast.

Both of my parents had taken the day off to be with me. My sister Mary ran around me while we ate. She was a beautiful little girl with long hair and was as excited to see me as I was to see her. She was three.

"I felt very adult in my uniform, and my parents were very proud of me. After breakfast, I got in my car that had been sitting in front of my parents' house and I drove by Selena's aunt's house. When I noticed a Ford with Mexican plates parked in front, I made a U-turn and pulled up behind it. My heart began to beat faster.

I sat in the car, staring at the Ford, then at the door. I knew that I should just drive away. I talked myself into it, started the car up, and left.

I drove a few blocks and circled back. I could not resist.

* * *

As I approached the door, it swung open, revealing Selena standing there. I froze in place, captivated by her presence. Though I have no memory of what she was wearing, I gazed at her long and hard. I had missed her so much, with little hope or expectation of seeing her again. A little smile graced her face and slowly transformed into a wide grin. The next thing I knew, we were embracing passionately. At first, we said nothing. I could taste the tears as they flowed down both our faces. Her aunt's kids crowded around us, and still, we hadn't exchanged a word.

Inside the house, her aunt greeted me with a hug and a kiss. The biggest surprise was that her long-estranged parents were there. Selena introduced me to her mother and father, who seemed somewhat old-fashioned, as she had described, almost as if they had stepped out of the fifties. Selena favored her good-looking mom, who was shorter than Selena. Her father, probably in his mid-forties, said very little but observed me closely in my Navy uniform, which the kids were still gawking over.

Selena then excused us and led me to the den, where she closed the door and then came into my arms.

"George, please don't hate me," she said. "I never intended to run away, but I needed to be certain. I had to see him again to understand my true feelings."

(She paused, looking into my eyes)

"How do you feel about him?" I asked.

"He was my boyfriend, and I have no regrets about not conforming to societal expectations. He doesn't genuinely care for me, and I realized that when we reunited in Juarez."

(We were perched on the edge of the sofa, turning to look at each other)

"Are you saying that you would choose him if he were ready to marry you, and now you realize that he just wants to play around, which is why you are disenchanted with him?" I asked.

(She let out a sigh)

"It's you that I love, and I'm not looking for us to marry," she paused. "But I will marry you if that's truly what you desire. I'm done with Sergio, just know that. I'm completely done with him."

(She then kissed me)

"I made peace with my parents and explained to them that I was in love with a young man from Los Angeles. I told them how I was very serious about you. I told them you had green eyes." She looked at me, gazing straight into my eyes as if she was checking to see if they were still green.

(She paused for a moment)

"I came back to my aunt's house, and I looked everywhere but couldn't find you. I called you, but your mother said you left school and had gone away. She did not tell me you went into the Navy. The drugstore owner didn't know how to contact you, but he said you had joined the navy and that you were probably in boot camp for a while."

"My mom should have told you how to write me," I said.

Selena brushed it off. "She's a mother. I get it. It's okay. I figured I would leave a letter here for you and called my parents to come to get me. They got here last night. The plan was I'd go back with them. They wanted to come and visit my aunt anyway, or I would have flown like I did when I left."

"Are you going back with them?"

"Do you want me to?"

I took her face in my hands and kissed her slowly and long.

"No, I don't want you to ever leave again." She put her arms around me. "I won't ever leave you again, ever!"

"Will you marry me?" I asked.

(A pause in which we are staring at each other up close)

"I will marry you if that's what you really want. If we don't get married right away, my parents will go back with the news that I eloped with an American and got married. That will make them both happy."

"Let's get married," I said.

There was a pause before she spoke again. Our stare fixed on each other.

"We don't need to get married for us to stay together. I don't want you to rush unless you really want to do it. At this point, my parents will accept us living together as long as we do it here and not in Juarez, where everyone knows us."

"I want to marry you," I said. I had never been more serious in my life.

"In that case, let's do it."

Chapter 10
The Promise of Forever

We exchanged vows in the cozy living room of my parents' home, once the residence of Thelma, the woman to whom I owed thirty-five hundred dollars.

The faint scent of fresh flowers mixed with the comforting aroma of tamales and mole wafted through the air, creating a sense of intimacy and love. As the preacher, a family friend, spoke the words of union, the sound of his gentle voice filled the room. The central heating system was on; it was a cold January day.

The tangible marriage certificate, handed to us by the preacher before he departed, symbolized not just a legal bond but also a bridge of understanding and acceptance with Selena's parents. Their preference was a Catholic marriage, but that was a promise for the future.

Lucky for us, I scored an extra two weeks of furlough from the Navy. (As they left for Juarez, Selena's dad handed her a wad of bills - $300 totaling 3,750 pesos, a sweet sum for our Mexican getaway.) We embarked on our honeymoon journey to Mexico City, a lengthy drive in my trusty Ford.

From the heartwarming reunion at her aunt's place to the swift departure for our honeymoon spot, it was a whirlwind. By the time we reached a roadside motel in Ontario on the first night, we were eager to make up for lost time. Ring or no ring, the thrill of being with Selena was as intense as always. The four-day non-stop drive to Mexico City ended with our arrival at the Ritz Hotel, making every moment of the journey worthwhile.

"I joined the Navy to get away when I thought you were gone for good. Now I don't know what to do. I don't want to go back," I told Selena on our honeymoon bed.

"Can't you get out?"

"I don't think I can get out."

Selena wrapped her naked body around me. "In that case, don't go back. My father can stake us in Juarez to open a business there."

"You don't want to live in the U.S. do ya?"

"I love Mexico. I'll live wherever you say."

"But you prefer Mexico, tell the truth." I chuckled.

She had a beautiful smile. "I prefer Mexico," she admitted.

"I love you, Selena."

"You took the words right out of my mouth," she said.

Chapter 11
Juarez, Mexico

As soon as we hit Juarez, my furlough extension called it quits. Going back to the San Diego Base was now a long shot. With the extension out of the picture, I was skating on thin ice, risking a stint in the brig for going AWOL. In the back of my mind, boot camp warnings about wartime desertion penalties – even death sentences – flashed like neon signs. AWOL, a lighter offense, still meant facing time locked up.

When Selena's dad got wind of my plan to settle in Juarez, he hooked me up with Julio Chavez, a lawyer he knew from El Paso. We kicked back into our motel room, just a stone's throw from the bed and the mini kitchen.

"So, you're turning eighteen in October, born in Mexico, and a U.S. citizen," Julio pointed out.

"Yeah, that's me," I confirmed.

"At eighteen, the ball's in your court. Stay a U.S. citizen, or give it up and choose to be a Mexican Citizen. Being a Mexico native gives you that choice. Go Mexican, and Uncle Sam might not rain on your parade for ditching the Navy. Any other worries, dude?"

Selena said, "Sorry for dragging you out here for such a quick chat. We could've just had a phone conversation."

Julio shrugged off the distance, saying, "Your pops wanted me here, so here I am. No sweat. It was a pleasure meeting George and seeing you again." They smiled at each other before he said. "She was a little girl when I first met her at her parent's residence."

We were up, and Julio was ready to exit. "This is a giant step. Think long and hard. You might want to return, settle out the AWOL, and find a way to get discharged. Once you do, come back and settle here." We shook hands. He kissed Selena on both cheeks and was out of the tiny room.

Somewhere, a quiet voice in my mind urged me to slow down and avoid rushing, but I disregarded it. My focus was on Selena, the love of my life, and the thought of being separated from her for four years in the Navy was unbearable.

I joined the Navy because of heartbreak, but that pain had vanished with Selena back in my life. I no longer had any desire to be a sailor. Reflecting on it now, if Selena had said, "Stay in the Navy; you have my full support." I would have seriously thought about continuing. I was in school training to be a hospital corpsman, a promising role. If I had remained in San Diego, I would have gone home each night like any regular job. I adored the uniforms, and once boot camp was behind me, it didn't seem too demanding.

Despite the senselessness of staying in Juarez, I resolved to remain. Downtown Juarez reminded me of Tijuana but on a grander scale, with dust filling the air and competing stores seeking to attract tourists from El Paso. Although Selena loved Juarez as her home, I knew this sentiment wouldn't sway my mother's disapproval.

I had to call my mom and explain my plans to stay in Juarez.

"You can't do that, George. Mexico is not a future for you."

"I have to, Mom. Do you want to see me in jail? I can't go back. At least not now. Let me find a way out of the Navy."

Not surprisingly, my mother's underlying disapproval surfaced, "I knew I didn't like that girl from the first day I met her!"

"Mom, this is on me, not her."

Selena's dad drove us around and showed us his available commercial rentals. Everything her dad said was with a tone of finality.

"You should open a grocery store. If it goes well, you can expand to a supermarket."

I put up no argument but didn't want to open a grocery store. One place he showed us was strategically positioned in the center of a block, with a small building adjacent to it and facing Plaza Bella Vista, just two hundred feet away from a Catholic Church.

I asked my father-in-law about the smaller building next to the potential market.

"Small for a grocery store," my father-in-law said. "I have a key if you want to take a look."

"Papa, let's see it," Selena said.

I learned that Selena's aunt, Carmen, owned the building.

As we toured the compact shop, it reminded me of my birthplace in Agua Prieta, Mexico, where my father owned a small curio store, and my mother operated a flower shop. We lived in the back of the stores, and I was born in one of those rooms.

Inspired by the bustling ice cream vendors in the plazita across the street. I spontaneously envisioned converting the building into an ice cream parlor. I imagined a Baskin-Robbins 31 Flavors store similar to the ones we have back home. I have a deep love for ice cream and often visit their stores.

"It doesn't take much," I told Selena and her father. A counter, freezers, and a place for people to sit and eat. Happy colors inside and out.

Selena said, [1]"¡Tienes toda la razón! He visitado un 31 Sabores antes, y sus tiendas están llenas de numerosos espejos. Happy tiene razón. Disfrutar de helado es absolutamente encantador. ¡Estoy emocionada por esto!"

Eventually, the father-in-law transitioned from initial displeasure to offering creative suggestions for setting up the ice cream parlor. This positive interaction with Selena's father marked a promising start to our new venture.

"What do you think, Selena? Will it work?"

She kissed me on the lips. "We can make it work," she said.

"We only sell ice cream and drinks," I said. "No food. Keep it simple. We serve big portions. Huge scoops on ice cream cones and yummy-looking ice cream dishes."

"Yes!" Selena agreed. "One suggestion."

"Tell us," I said, excited.

"Many youngsters around here are like us. They love rock and roll. We need a jukebox filled with current and old hits."

Before I could comment, her father said. "A nickel per play. I have vending machines all over town. I can get a new jukebox for you."

---

1. "You're absolutely right! I've visited 31 Flavors, and their stores are filled with numerous mirrors. Happy is spot on. Indulging in ice cream is absolutely delightful. I'm thrilled about this!"

I beamed. I wasn't about to ask him how much of a cut he wanted from each nickel. "Am I correct that our prices will be in pesos?"

"Pesos," Selena said. Her father nodded.

"Then how will we get away with a nickel per play?"

"Even beggars have a nickel." Her father said this.

This time, Selena nodded in agreement.

"Amor. The good news is that good and bad people will buy our ice cream and spend their nickels playing rock and roll in our jukebox. The bad news is that this is the roughest neighborhood in Juarez. People get killed right across the street at the plazita all the time. You need to consider this.

Her father shook his head. "Not that bad. We have lived here for many years. Everyone knows the family. You will be safe."

"We lived here until Papa built the new house in another neighborhood. He's right. Everyone knows us. Even the very bad people like us. Still, you need to know."

"Sounds like you don't have a problem then?"

"I don't have a problem at all. You need to feel the same."

"I'm in," I said. "Can we meet with your aunt about renting this place? I'm dying to know how much the rent is."

"You would have been better off renting one of my places," my father-in-law said.

"My aunt is a lovely person. Papa. Don't be mean." Laughs.

Having been raised in East LA, which was no walk in the park, I navigated through it all. Memories flood my mind of Pi, my friend, along with his crew and the rest of the gangs, seated on makeshift chairs in our clubhouse, which was once my garage, glued to a small TV screen. I have a knack for getting along with everyone.

As we approached Carmen's house, Selena pointed out all the adjacent properties her aunt owned. Most were one-story apartments connected one after another. I was more impressed by the inside of the old house. It was modern and comfortable, decorated in shades of brown, with two rugged bearskin rugs on the living room floor.

Carmen embraced Selena, kissing her on both cheeks. "Congratulations, my dear!"

Then Carmen gave me a big hug and did a double kiss. "Congratulations, George. I hope it's okay to call you by your first name." I liked her immediately. She was a big woman with a hot body. Great looks like Selena's family. Oh, and she smelled great!

"Of course, it's fine. You call me George."

The aroma of something in the oven permeated the air deliciously.

"Tia, what are you baking?"

"Marcela is baking pan dulce."

"We got here just in time!" Selena said.

"I am delighted you did. Let's go to the kitchen; we can eat and talk there."

Selena and I followed Carmen into the inviting kitchen, where Marcella, the skilled baker, warmly welcomed us. Before we settled around the intricately carved wooden table, Marcella kindly took our jackets, ensuring our comfort in the cozy warmth of the kitchen. The stark contrast between the chilly exterior and the toasty atmosphere inside made the kitchen a comforting refuge from the cold outside.

Within minutes of our arrival, Marcela started serving hot Mexican chocolate and the freshly made pan dulce.

Carmen learned why we were there. "Are you truly committed to not returning to the United States?"

"Absolutely. I'm already absent without leave. Going back

now would result in a court-martial and, without a doubt, jail."

Carmen said, "I can't imagine you would get too harsh of a sentence for overstaying a short time."

"Tia. he's not going back."

"Okay. I believe you." She took a bite and a sip.

"We like your building. We're hoping you will rent it to us."

Carmen smiled.

"Of course - I will rent the building to you. Do you have the money to fix it up to meet your requirements?"

"Papa said he'd loan us the money."

Carmen handed me a pencil and a pad.

"Give me a breakdown of all expenses you anticipate," Carmen said.

"Aunt Carmen, he's not familiar with the prices here."

"In that case, write everything you need to open the store. I will rent the building and loan you the money to fix it how you want it."

"Tia, that's very nice of you."

"Too nice," I added. "Are you sure?"

"I'm sure."

Selena chuckled with glee. "In that case, Tia - we'll get to the list right now."

My brain retrieved a picture of a 31 Flavors Store, and I started writing. Selena leaned over my shoulder to check my hurried scribbles on the notepad. A gentle kiss on my head surprised me, and Carmen's delighted clap followed this unexpected gesture. "You are such a lovely couple!"

"Adoro a este hombre[2]."

"We need a carpenter," I said. "The counter, cabinets, maybe the tables and chairs. Do you know someone?"

Carmen didn't answer. "Marcela, go find Pancho and tell him to get over here right now."

"Uncle Pancho?" Selena asked.

"Yes, the one and only. He's a drunk, but he's the best carpenter in Juarez. He wastes his time doing body and fender work when he could be out building for a lot more money. He hasn't paid me rent in months. He'll do this."

Pancho was a formidable presence with hands like bear paws, radiating strength and power. Standing tall at over six feet, he commanded attention with his rugged and imposing demeanor. Upon entering Carmen's kitchen, his expression hinted at a depth of emotion, which shifted instantly upon laying eyes on Selena. His face transformed into a wide, beaming smile as he approached her. With a gentle touch, he lifted her from the chair, showering affectionate kisses on each cheek. Selena giggled with delight, holding onto him tightly. Laughter

---

2. I adore this man.

filled the room as we all joined in; Carmen and Marcela caught up in the infectious joy of the moment.

I was introduced to Pancho. He sat at the table where we were and declined Marcela's offer of hot chocolate but reached for a pan dulce right off.

Selena started discussing why we needed him on our project. A short while later, we all walked two blocks to the building. Pancho was the only one who did not wear a jacket. "Soon, the temperature will be steaming hot," he told us.

"Tio, that's not today. It's cold out here right now."

Pancho Laughed at Selena's remark. [3]"Presidente keeps me warm." Laughing.

"Pancho, I have a vision for the ice cream parlor layout. Picture this - as you walk into the store, there will be 10 small tables with chairs, each seating four customers. Along one side, there will be a long counter that spans the width of the space, where people can order and pick up their ice cream. We'll have stools affixed to the floor for seating. Behind this counter, we'll have freezers for ice cream and reach-in soda coolers. And, there will be a second counter behind the first one for the shake blenders and supplies we use for the sales like cones and plastic dishes."

Selena and I are walking with Pancho through the space.

---

3. Presidente is a brandy made in Mexico.

Carmen is standing at a distance, but I see she is listening.

"And Pancho, here's the kicker - the rooms in the back of the store will be transformed into living quarters. One room will be our bedroom, complete with a toilet and space for a shower, all tiled. The adjacent big room will be a storage haven with plenty of shelves for supplies like cups, ice cream dishes, cones, and napkins. I know there's more to consider as we venture into the ice cream parlor business, and with your expertise, I am confident we can make this a success. What do you think, Pancho? I stopped talking because I was out of ideas.

"I can do it."

Carmen said, "he's a drunk, but he can do anything."

"Don't be so mean to Tio," Selena said with a chuckle.

"The woman is crazy; I pay no mind to what she says."

Selena said, "Tio, we need hot water. Can't live here without it."

He nodded. "I take care of that."

"I don't think you should live here," Carmen said, looking at Selena. We are all standing around. There is no place to sit in the space.

"Tia, it's okay. We can always move later."

"Does your father know you plan to live in the back of the business?"

"Tia, I didn't know until a few minutes ago," laughing.

"I'm sorry," I said. "We don't have to live here."

Selena walked over to me and playfully poked my chest. "I'll live with you anywhere, Amor." She kissed me. Pancho whistled. Carmen clapped.

We returned to Carmen's house, and Pancho agreed to start working immediately. "I will draw a rough draft tonight and show it to you tomorrow."

"Perfect," I said.

After Pancho left we settled on a rental amount with Carmen and she gave Selena and I an envelope with twenty-five-thousand pesos. Two Thousand Dollars.

Selena gave her Tia a big hug. "Gracias, gracias."

"This is way too fast. Thank you for your trust," I said.

I drove us to the motel we were staying in on the outskirts of Juarez. It was a new place with nice rooms, a great swimming pool and prices were cheap.

"I worry about borrowing money," I said. "I don't want your aunt to become my victim like Thelma."

"Stop worrying about it. We have my father to back us if we need him."

"You don't get it," I said.

"Amor, I do get it. You're worried that a loan might turn out like the one you couldn't repay to your girlfriend's mother. But this time, it's different - the money is for starting a business, not hiring a crook lawyer to get your brother out of jail."

She embraced me tightly, showering me with kisses. A few minutes later, our clothes were off, and we fell onto the bed.

Later, as we sat on the disheveled bed, I said, "No need to involve your dad with loans for us."

"Okay, Amor, whatever you say. Relax. The parlor is going to be a hit. The jukebox will pull it off."

"First profits go to your aunt. I want her paid fast."

"Amor, whatever you say is fine with me."

I knew one thing for certain. If I ever met up with that lawyer in Mexico who had scammed my mom, I would kick his ass.

Selena seemed to think her father was a bottomless supply of money. Sure, he appeared to be solvent, but he wasn't rich. He drove a two-year-old Ford. If I were rich, I'd have a garage full of sports cars.

I nurtured a deep aspiration to achieve success independently and accumulate my first million. Yet, the stark reality of my situation loomed large. Here I was, AWOL from the Navy, stranded in the remote expanse of Mexico, relying on borrowed funds to make ends meet. Reflecting on the days of doing yard work with Pi and even earlier, I had a savings account and a steady income stream—even at ten. Now, approaching 18, I found myself without a savings account and no source of income until the ice cream parlor opened. My aspirations hinged on the business's success, creating a sense of uncertainty. Despite receiving accolades for my intellect, I couldn't help but feel the weight of my present predicament. I grappled with these thoughts alone, contemplating the path ahead with humility.

The following weeks kept Selena and me on our toes. Juarez's leading ice cream maker graciously lent us two new freezers and a batch of promotional items in return for our commitment to purchasing their ice cream. Coca-Cola also stepped in, providing us with soda refrigerators and a dispenser. Selena's father came through with a new jukebox, agreeing to take a quarter of the machine's earnings instead of a direct payment, which was a better arrangement. The coin slot was calibrated for a US nickel, roughly equivalent to sixty cents in pesos, the price of a single scoop ice cream cone.

A talented sign painter adorned the front of the building with price lists and images of delectable ice cream creations. One striking feature was the snow-capped Mount Everest he painted on the plate glass window, with the cap cleverly resembling a scoop of ice cream. At that moment and even now, I remain puzzled about what led me to choose "El Keno" for the shop.

Amidst the exhilaration of seeing our business take shape exactly as Selena and I envisioned, an overwhelming sense of stress weighed on me. I felt burdened far beyond my years, grappling with the thought of Thelma and the debts I owed her. The realization that I couldn't simply cross the border into the United States without risking severe repercussions loomed over me, stirring a profound sense of helplessness and regret.

As night fell and I retired to bed with my wife Selena, our intimate moments became a sanctuary, offering respite from the weight of my worries and the relentless stress.

Chapter 12
Fast Friends

Selena and I strolled through the bustling plazita across from the ice cream parlor, immersing ourselves in the vibrant atmosphere, seemingly unaffected by the gentle warmth in the air. The pleasant weather created a welcoming ambiance as we meandered around. Despite the late afternoon hour, a cool breeze lingered, hinting at the approaching nighttime chill. Instead of grass, we walked among a few tall trees scattered here and there. The plaza was adorned with numerous park benches, offering a respite for the casually gathered crowds while children joyfully played around, adding to the lively spirit. The air was filled with the tempting aroma of roasting corn on the cob and the cheerful melodies emanating from the ice cream vendor's mobile freezer, heightening the buzz and chatter that filled the square.

Selena, who was familiar with everyone we met, and I enthusiastically lobbied the soon-to-be-open ice cream shop, conversing with the local inhabitants. Amid this, Selena softly nudged my shoulder, diverting my focus from the animated exchange to two individuals who could have used Ambrose's skill in providing a five-dollar haircut back in East Los Angeles. These men were thrilled to see Selena back in Juarez, warmly welcoming her excitedly. Despite their messy looks, they radiated a friendly aura as they eagerly shook my hand, continuing their warm greetings for several minutes.

"This is Keno, my husband," she introduced me.

"Who the hell is Keno?" I asked with a chuckle.

"Amor, that's you," laughing. Lion and Tigre patted my back with approval and chuckled. "The name of your [1] Neveria," offered Lion.

From that point forward, I was known as Keno to everyone. Enough people were talking around us simultaneously, and I didn't catch the names of the last two guys. Selena clarified for me. They were two of her childhood friends, Lion and Tigre.

"They're grandsons of Perla."

"Perla?" The name didn't trigger any recognition.

"And who exactly is Perla?" I inquired.

Selena unraveled the tales of a notorious figure in Mexico, known as Perla but born Magda Hidalgo. Her

---

1. Ice Cream Store

alias reverberated across the streets of Mexico with an intimidating presence that resonated deeply.

Perla, a striking seventy-year-old, reigned as a renowned drug lord within the confines of a colossal estate encompassing an entire city block, shielded by towering twelve-foot walls and fortified by unwavering political alliances, granting her immunity from legal interventions.

"She's not just a mere figurehead," Selena continued, "Perla embodies a paradox of benevolence and power. Despite her daunting reputation, she harbors a philanthropic side. Owning hundreds of apartments, she graciously offers shelter to destitute families free of charge. Her generosity extends to a public swimming pool and a round-the-clock bakery, serving the needy with unlimited access to essentials. From complimentary coffee, bread, and pastries to providing milk for children in need—her benevolent acts transcend mere charity." Selena paused, hinting at the depth of Perla's generosity. "And that's just the beginning."

"Have you ever met her?" I asked.

"It was some time ago," Selena replied. "Her nephews introduced me to her. She appears classy and rich with fancy jewelry - gold necklaces, gemstones, and numerous rings. No one would dare to rob her," Selena laughed. She may seem ordinary at first, but there's a mysterious and captivating aura about her. People talk a lot about her intriguing personality."

"What kind of stories?"

"There's a tale about a furnace in her basement where supposedly she cremates those who have betrayed or owe her dealers money."

"I find that hard to believe," I responded.

"Amor, I believe all the rumors, always have."

I commented to Selena, "Her nephews look like wrestlers. They're both over six feet and big."

"Speaking of size, Uncle Pancho is even larger," she reminded me. "Perla raised them, and they received schooling from a private tutor at home."

"What about their parents?"

"Rumors suggest their mother died of an overdose while their father's cause of death remains unclear. This tragedy occurred when Lion and Tigre were just infants. Perla took on the responsibility of raising them, and their reputation strikes fear among people, resembling that of Perla. There are rumors of their involvement in the deaths of at least four individuals who owed money for drugs. Reporters who spread such tales often meet unfortunate fates. Some reporters were found…" She paused, glancing around. "Over there," she pointed with uncertainty. "No, there," she corrected herself.

"You've been watching too many gangster movies," I teased.

"Amor, I grew up in a world filled with gangsters. This area is rife with gunslingers and their territories," she explained, gesturing to our surroundings.

"So, why are they freely roaming about?"

"Perla's influence and wealth hold sway here. Additionally, who would dare to come forward as a witness?"

"I can tell they sure like you."

"Yes, they like me, and I like them very much."

"Crazy names," I offered.

"Lion's name is Rico Santos, and Tigre is Victor Santos."

"Thanks," I said. "What a WoW story about Perla."

"People fear her, but they love her. Does that make sense to you?"

"If it makes sense to you, it makes sense to me." I hugged my wife, and we kissed passionately. We were sitting on a bench at the plazita. Directly across the street was our Neveria.

Chapter 13
El Keno

Before the grand opening, my friendship with Tigre and Lion blossomed, establishing them as loyal confidants. Their presence in the ice cream parlor maintained peace, deterring younger patrons from loitering around the jukebox when older churchgoers visited for a sweet treat. The nearby church, with its perpetual masses, contributed significantly to our customer base.

To enhance our ice cream expertise, we enlisted Jose, a seasoned worker from a Juarez ice cream parlor, to guide us in creating a delectable menu. While Selena meticulously transcribed the recipes, I photographed each signature treat. Meanwhile, Pancho skillfully repaired the HVAC units that kept the entire establishment cool, except for our living quarters.

Upon completing the carpentry, including a discreet storage wall concealed behind a curtain, Pancho took charge of the painting duties. Our window artist-adorned metal signs with picturesque ice cream delights adorn the walls with a tantalizing display. With our preparations in place, we were poised for the grand opening.

Following a two-day intensive training with Jose, he generously extended his assistance for future needs. Subsequently, Selena and I delved into perfecting our creations, procuring recommended serving dishes and essential supplies that the ice cream factory overlooked. Selena ventured across the border to El Paso for American-made staples like waffle cones, napkins, straws, cups, cherries, and toppings, a task I regrettably couldn't join her due to the risk involved.

A couple of nights before the grand opening, we gathered for a special dinner at Selena's Aunt Carmen's place, as our hotel room would have been far too small to accommodate such a large family gathering. The cozy bungalow we called temporary home, offering a significant upgrade from our past motel experiences in California, featured a bathroom, a modest kitchen, and a bedroom furnished with a generous king-size bed, complemented by a comfy sofa and a television set where we relaxed after the meal. Despite the relatives' reservations about our prolonged stay in a hotel, our focus remained unwavering on finalizing the preparations for the ice cream parlor's grand opening under Pancho's expert guidance, ensuring everything was primed for the big day.

"Wait till they digest that we are leaving the hotel and

going to live in the back of the business," I said with a chuckle.

"Amor. They all know it, but they haven't digested it yet."

Selena and I didn't want to stay in the hotel forever or in the back rooms of the store. It would be nice to have a place of our own, but it was important that I pay our way. The last thing I wanted was to make more debt.

"Where are you going to live then?" Luna asked.

"We're going to move into the back rooms at our business," Selena announced.

Luna was 18. Of all the sisters, she was the only one who did not have fair European coloring and light eyes. Her eyes were a dark brown, her brows at a sharper angle than Selena's, and she was mature-looking. Her skin was fair but more like honey than buttermilk. I ignored her full hips, flat stomach, and large breasts. She was my sister-in-law.

Selena dedicated twenty-four hours to turning the ice cream parlor's two back rooms into a cozy retreat. Our bedroom was a collection of heartfelt gifts—a mismatched bed and bureau from different aunts, an oversized chair from yet another, and Pancho's added touch of small shelves doubling as nightstands.

The bedding told its own tale—silk sheets, plump pillows, and a vibrant comforter, all carefully selected by my wife during a trip to El Paso, presented as a thoughtful gift from her mother, complete with an extra set of sheets and pillowcases.

As Selena finished transforming our sleeping space, our bedroom in the back of the ice cream parlor radiated a warm and inviting ambiance. I never looked at Selena's bedroom at her parents' house, but I imagined it was classy. I saw the accommodations at her aunt's house in Los Angeles; they were clean but run-down. I'd say that the ice cream parlor accommodations were much better than where she was staying when I met her.

Our second room was barren except for our empty refrigerator."

"Are you okay living in the back of the store like this?" It was not the first time I asked her; it would not be the last time.

"I'm with you, and I'm in Mexico. I love it," Selena replied. "Mexico City wasn't built in a day. This is the beginning."

"I'll miss the pool at the hotel," I said.

Selena took my hand and kissed it. "We can rent a room when we want to get away, easy."

I nodded in agreement. It was the newest motel in all of Juarez. It wasn't cheap. It wasn't expensive. We got a great deal while there because we paid a week at a time.

* * *

Back to the ice cream parlor. Our first day was a big hit. We opened at ten in the morning and planned to stay open until midnight. Selena's parents and Carmen arrived early that evening and seemed impressed at everything but our living quarters. People came in groups. Most were in a party mood. We were down to our last scoop of vanilla at ten in the evening but stayed open until one that first night for our full house. The jukebox never stopped playing its repertoire of American Rock n' Roll. This made money for us and Selena's father, who got a slice of every nickel.

Selena got on the phone with the ice cream company the next morning about getting another freezer. They stocked our two freezers, installed a third one, and packed it full. Pancho had to install additional electric circuit breakers to handle the extra load on the existing outlets. The man could do everything.

I dialed the Coke Company. They picked up the line as Selena walked up with the keys to one of her father's cars. She jingled them in my face, giggling. I had to put my hand over the phone.

"I'll be back with a car so full of supplies, we will not run out again," she said. Then she took off for El Paso, nine miles away, with one of her father's pickups trailing behind her.

Coca-Cola couldn't get around to stocking us in time to do us any good. I called Pepsi and told them about our success the night before and that I needed beverages immediately. The Coke refrigerators were moved out. Pepsi moved new ones in and stocked us up. All done in a matter of a few hours.

After the Pepsi guys left, Selena got back with the supplies. The driver who had followed her to El Paso had packed the pickup full. We packed in as much as possible in a rush and tried to figure out where to put the rest. There were boxes and backup items everywhere, filling up our storage area and in full view. The second day, all the disposable cups were leaning against a wall behind the counter. They came in twelve-foot stacks inside tall cardboard boxes. We crammed ten feet of cups in four feet of space. They were too tall for the low ceiling on that wall, and they kept toppling over.

Selena and I worked behind the counter, preparing orders. Our two helpers, Nacho and Cuco, had been trained by Jose. They waited on tables and cleaned up. Business was better than good. The place was a madhouse packed with customers day and night. It was a small-time money maker. Nickels and dimes, but lots of them.

Selena got to where she was turning bright red as she picked the boxes up for the hundredth time and leaned them against the wall, only to knock them over the next time she went by. When everyone was gone that night, I carried the cups and boxes into our kitchen–if an empty room with an empty refrigerator can be called a kitchen.

"This is our new storeroom," I said.

"You genius!" Selena squealed and leaped across the room like she was training to be a cat. She fixed her arms around my neck.

"You must hate living back here," I told Selena.

"That again? I would tell you if I hated it. It's fun. Look how fit I am."

"I dare you to strip so I can see."

Selena stripped and did a three-sixty. The hard work showed on her body. I took her bent over a big box of happy clown cones.

"You're an exhibitionist," I said.

"Nobody was watching but you," she said.

"You like to be watched." She got excited when I talked to her like that, and I got excited seeing her excited.

"Next time, you want to leave the door open?" she asked. "I am as much an exhibitionist as the next person, and so are you, Keno."

"I am not. I want to please you."

She laughed. "Sure, you do. Let's do it at the plaza. Want to?"

"Yeah, right, the Plaza. The church people will stone us.

We joked around a lot.

Selena's father frequently meddled. Selena dealt with him gently. He advocated hiring more staff, but we resisted. Selena and I never grumbled about the long hours. Our hard work enabled us to repay Carmen the money she loaned us forty-five days after our opening. Until then, we hired two extra employees to assist our team during the bustling night shifts. The one thing our neighborhood had in abundance was poverty, yet there was always an American nickel or dime for an ice cream cone, milkshake, or banana split. And for those who couldn't afford it, we often treated them. This was especially true for the elderly who visited after church or for the children I noticed peering through the large window. I would step out with a basket of ice cream cones and distribute them. The joy on their faces was priceless.

"You keep that up, we're going to go broke," Selena teased.

"No, we won't. What goes around, comes around."

We kissed.

"I was kidding," she said.

"I know you were kidding."

* * *

Pancho had constructed an abundance of tables and chairs for our space. El Keno had become a beloved local hotspot. Long queues formed, particularly at night, as everyone vied for a spot. With limited table space, patrons were eager to be part of the musical experience. Those unable to secure a table ordered and either moved outside or mingled around, ensuring the establishment remained bustling. The vibrant ambiance, amplified by the music, made it an exceptionally lively scene.

We had a propane stove on a tabletop in the storeroom/kitchen, but we didn't cook. When we got hungry, we walked to a restaurant. There were many places within walking distance where we could eat. Selena knew where and where not to eat—especially not in our so-called kitchen. Makeshift as it was, it was the pits, and the shower wasn't great either. It was an add-on and hadn't been plumbed very well. We rushed Pancho to do it quickly when we were about to have our grand opening.

I was okay with it, but I didn't believe Selena when she claimed to be okay. We had no television. We did have the jukebox. If we turned it on before we were open, a crowd of kids crossed the plaza to listen. We could have purchased a TV and installed an antenna on the roof, something we had discussed but didn't do. We were busy selling ice cream and fooling around with each other. There was really no time to watch television.

During the day, we took a break during slow periods and let one of the day workers take over. We'd go out to eat, return to lie down, grab a quickie, and snooze for a little bit. We could not get enough of each other. After closing, we usually walked four blocks to the all-night restaurant, where they specialized in every flauta imaginable with flour or corn tortillas. They served the flautas cut in two-inch pieces topped with guacamole, *pico de gallo,* and other choices.

Even at night, the streets and sidewalks teemed with people after closing the store. We often heard friendly catcalls from familiar faces. In the dark plaza, the glow of marijuana joints flickered like fireflies. (Back in the USA, possession of just one joint could land you in prison.) In a way, you could get high just by taking a walk. It felt like living in a devil's den, yet Selena and I felt immune and protected from the dark surrounding danger. For a while, despite exhaustion, we were very content. I was accustomed to hard work—the drugstore had demanded many hours of my life. In comparison, our ice cream parlor was demanding to the extreme because it was our own, and business was booming.

Smoking Marijuana in Mexico was also a crime, but in the time I was there, I never heard of an arrest.

Chapter 14
The Feds

I called home every ten days or so. One week, my mother told me the FBI had come looking for me. I never asked her if she gave them my address and phone number.

Two weeks later, when the parlor was as full as ever, four strangers walked into our ice cream parlor while Selena and I were busy behind the counter. The patrons suddenly stopped eating and talking, yet the jukebox kept playing as they tried to listen to what was going on. It was obvious that everyone knew the visitors were police.

"Who are those men?" Selena asked. "They look like police. The Mexicans are Feds for sure."

As they all looked in my direction, Lion and Tigre entered and shook hands with the two Mexicans. The two Americans shook hands, too, and just listened. The jukebox was too loud for me to hear anything. After a few minutes, they walked out together. In a few minutes more, Tigre came back alone.

I leaned over the counter and whispered, "FBI?"

He grinned. "Two Mexican Federales, and two FBI. We know the local feds. The FBI wants to talk to you. They are not here to arrest you," he whispered urgently. He glanced at the boisterous crowd enjoying their ice cream and the jukebox music. Although it was daylight, it was an unusually rowdy crowd for an ice cream parlor. "And between you and me, they wouldn't be able to get you out of here if they tried," he added with a wry grin.

The tension grew thicker as the patrons strained to catch snippets of the conversation. It was clear that everyone was keenly aware of the presence of the law enforcement officers.

"He is not going to see them, Tigre," Selena said quietly, wiping whipped cream from her fingers. She hopped up to perch on the edge of the tall stool we kept on our side of the counter, tucking the cloth she'd used to wipe down the freezer box into the apron around her waist. There was an unusual calmness about her, an eerie quiet before the storm.

"It won't hurt anything to talk," Tigre said, trying to maintain a sense of nonchalance. "The local feds are with them because the FBI has no authority."

Selena's golden eyes flashed. Her voice raised, and she jumped to her feet, facing Tigre with her arms akimbo, and her hands balled up into fists, her cheeks burning red with fury.

"He doesn't have to see them! I don't care what you-"

The jukebox was between songs. The room fell almost silent. All ears were pointed in our direction.

"Wait, honey," I said. "Calm down. Tigre is not the enemy. He is only trying to help out here."

Tigre nodded. He smiled at Selena. "Temper, temper, friend," he said.

Juarez, or at least the neighborhood where we lived, had that small-town vibe fueled by gossip. The area teemed with people listening in to catch the latest scoop. A soft murmur of conversation enveloped our customers as they chattered about the suited-up Americans now outside with the two Mexican cops, accompanied by Lion. I lowered my voice.

"Did they say what they want to talk about?" I asked.

Tigre shrugged. "Locals wouldn't lie to my brother and me. Talk only is what they said."

Selena said. "My father's lawyer explained your options. They can't extradite you just because you left the Navy. The Americans, they have no authority here. You didn't kill anyone."

The lawyer Julio didn't quite tell me what she was now saying. My options came when I turned eighteen, close by but not there yet. Julio didn't say they couldn't extradite me. He said they probably wouldn't extradite me.

"I'll go outside and talk to them." Taking off my apron, unbuttoned the shirt I wore while working and stepped out from behind the counter in my tee. "I'll handle this."

I felt a tug as Selena caught my hand. I looked at her face. Her hair was pinned back, and a couple of rebellious curls circled her forehead like a halo. She was lovely and very upset. Her color was high, and her expression was both vulnerable and angry.

"I'm going with you," she said, trailing behind me and Tigre. She neither released my hand nor stopped arguing. "You don't have to see them. Outside, you have no way of preventing them from taking you."

Tigre said,[1] "Selena, cálmate, no lo van a arrestar. Confía en mí."

The three of us stepped outside. Selena held onto me tightly as if I were her lifeline. Meanwhile, Tigre and Lion strolled to the adjacent building and leaned against its wall. Tigre casually lit a cigarette and engaged in conversation with his brother. They positioned themselves at a distance where they were not part of our discussion but near enough to intervene if they chose to do so.

I'd been in our air-conditioned place all day and felt pretty cool. The Americans had to be burning up in those suits. One of them mopped his face with a handkerchief.

---

1. Selena, calm down. They are not going to arrest him. Trust me.

The blonde must have been made of ice because he hadn't even broken a sweat.

"We're from the El Paso Federal Bureau. We're not here to arrest you, just to talk," the blonde American said, displaying his identification.

If they were from El Paso, about nine short miles away, they were locals from Texas, and you would think they would be acclimated to the weather.

I extended my right hand and shook hands with the Mexican cops first, then with the FBI agents.

"I'm all ears," I said.

"Want to talk here or in there?" the sweaty American agent asked.

He was probably hoping for air conditioning.

"Yes, here. There are too many customers inside."

Selena stepped up, holding my hand the whole time.

"I'm his wife. Why are you in Juarez? This is not your jurisdiction."

One of the Mexican agents said, "That's why we are here with them." He spoke very politely.

The FBI Agents ignored Selena. Their eyes were on me.

"There's a warrant for your arrest for being absent without leave from the Navy. You are aware of that?"

I nodded. "I am now," I said. "My mom said you went to see her. She did not mention a warrant."

"We didn't see your mother," the blonde agent said. "But agents in Los Angeles visited your parents, yes. Mr. Hatcher, we plan to return with extradition papers thirty days from today. You have two things you can do to prevent this. You can return to the US voluntarily or visit the American Embassy here in Juarez and renounce your US citizenship."

Selena's hand clutched tighter with every sentence from the agent's mouth. It was like her hand was screaming, *no, no, no!*

"I have to be eighteen to do that, right?"

"You'll be eighteen in less than three weeks. You were born in Mexico. You have the right to pick your nationality. If you renounce your US citizenship, we won't make any further attempts to extradite you. The US Attorney told me to make this very clear to you."

"I understand."

"Here's my card if you want more information or you decide to come back to the US. It will be safer to call us to take you back than to get caught on the other side where you'll be subject to arrest."

"I have no plans of going back."

The blonde agent sighed and looked at me sadly. He was an older guy, probably my dad's age, tanned dark, and the wrinkles around his bright eyes were lighter than his browned face. He looked sympathetic. "That's too bad, son. You're making a mistake, but it's your life."

I politely extended my hand to the FBI guys and then to the Mexican cops.

"Thank you for coming," I said.

We all smiled at each other, except for Selena, who glared at everyone.

Tigre and Lion huddled briefly with the two Mexican agents, shook hands, and the four men walked away. No telling where their cars were parked.

"I'm sorry that I'm such a bitch," Selena said, then kissed me.

Tigre and Lion stood there watching us, and then we all walked back into the busy store.

I thanked Tigre and Lion.

"You're very welcome, Keno. Did you think we wanted you to leave? Where would we go for fun if you left?"

I didn't have a license to sell alcohol. Selling alcohol without a license was a serious offense in Mexico. Our refrigerator still had no food, but it had beer, technically for Selena and me. We kept it for Tigre and Lion and served it to them with a straw in the large white cups we kept for milkshakes to go.

"Thank you, Tigre, Lion," Selena said. "Sorry if I was grouchy with you."

Tigre laughed and sipped his beer, not using the straw, which was there for appearances only. [2]"You've always been Resongona."

Lion added, "Bossy Selena since we were brats." We all laughed.

I laughed by reflex.

My brain had been tossed into a fog by the crisis. Sure, Spanish had been my first language, but I was an LA boy. I was American. I was Californian. I was an East Angeleno, for sure. If I renounced my citizenship, what would I be, other than an outcast, out of the USA forever? Is that what I wanted?

As Tigre and Lion finished their beer and left, I signaled Nacho to take charge of the order counter.

The space was filled with the laughter and chatter of our customers enjoying their favorite frozen treats. The jukebox in the corner blared out classic Rock and Roll tunes selected by our patrons, adding to the vibrant atmosphere. It was business as usual. Late afternoon.

We entered our bedroom, tucked away in the back of the parlor, finding solace amidst the distant sounds of the shop. Despite the constant hum of conversation and music, the bedroom offered a private retreat, shielded from prying eyes by the hustle and bustle of the business.

I reached for the bottle of Presidente I had set aside for

---

2. Whiny or Complainer

Pancho, seeking a moment of respite in the bedroom. The taste of the brandy contrasted with the room's warmth, enveloped in the scent of freshly made waffle cones and sweet ice cream flavors, far removed from the lively atmosphere of the parlor.

Selena winked at me.

"Hey, Mister, you want to play doctor? I have vaginal discomfort. Examine me, please."

This feeling I knew better. I lay down on the bed.

"You're so cute and sexy," I said, pushing the whole fiasco with the feds to the back of my mind.

Selena's comforting presence eased the discordance of the noisy surroundings as she rolled on top of me. The Rock and Roll melodies seeped through the walls, blending with the soft murmur of voices and the clinking of dishes from the parlor. In that moment, amidst the chaos and melody of our unconventional living arrangement, I found a sense of peace and belonging next to Selena.

Chapter 15
Pancho's Body Shop

In his laborer attire, Pancho always seemed like a puzzle to me. That evening, I decided to visit his simple body shop alone. Despite his tough exterior, I sensed a hidden side to him – one that was observant and understanding. I needed to talk to someone who would listen and offer thoughtful insight.

During his time at the ice cream parlor, Pancho would often make light of the challenging life he shared with Selena's Aunt Eliza. I knew they were renting from Carmen, the more affluent sister. Pancho's shop was a modest establishment by American standards, scarcely larger than a single-car garage. When he worked on a paint job, there was no room for bodywork. The space allowed for either painting or bodywork but not both at the same time. If he undertook a complete paint job or spot paint, he had to thoroughly clean up the area, washing down the ceiling, walls, and floor to mitigate dust.

Upon reaching his shop, I found Pancho had just completed painting an old Chevrolet. His makeshift spray booth consisted of four large pieces of plastic hanging from the ceiling, and a young kid outside was watering the dirt floor to quell the paint fumes and dust. As I entered, the lingering fume cloud bore testament to the freshly finished work.

Pancho was busily inspecting the Chevy as I arrived, his glistening, tanned skin adorned with a thin layer of perspiration. In one hand, he clutched a bottle of Presidente and, upon catching sight of me, he bellowed a warm greeting.

In the short time I had known him during his work at the ice cream parlor, my fondness for him had grown considerably. I genuinely liked him."Keno, come in. Have a drink!"

He passed me the bottle. It had wet paint handprints all over it. I grabbed it by the neck where it was cleanest and took a big drink. The heat of the liquor burned straight through me down to my toes. Drinking this brandy always did that to me.

Pancho laughed heartily and slammed my back.

"That is powerful shit, isn't it?" he shouted.

He was so loud that the forest of tools hanging from the

walls rattled in tune with his voice. At least, I thought they did.

I gasped for air and almost knocked off my feet. I wondered if Pancho's handprint had transferred to my shirt.

He took a long drink and returned the bottle to me. I shook my head, squinting and tearing up.

"Suit yourself," he said, tipping the bottle into his mouth.

He spoke of his wife, who had let herself go and was now obese. Her front teeth had been taken out, with no effort to get a dental plate made. She had little interest in her appearance. Pancho believed she fit the stereotype of the young and beautiful woman who becomes overweight after her first child, losing her looks. He claimed that one reason he drank was to escape his reality, and by the time he got to bed, he was so inebriated that his wife looked as beautiful to him as she did when he married her. Pancho shared this as if it were a big joke. I don't think he ever meant for me to pity him, but deep down, he was hurting. (Perhaps he wasn't hurting. I really don't know.) To me, his wife was overweight, but she was extremely pretty, just like Selena's mother, her sister, and Carmen, her other sister. As for missing teeth, I didn't see the evidence several times when Selena and I were with his wife.

He dusted off a spot for me to sit.

"What do you think of the paint job?" he asked.

I admired the car and then sat on the stool he'd wiped off next to the compressor. Spacious it wasn't, but I was comfortable there. It was just Pancho and me, but in a way it reminded me of the garage behind my apartment, where my friends and I had gathered.

"What brings you down here?" he asked.

"I just wanted to get away from the parlor for a while. Some days it's not fun."

"That's because you and my baby work like fools. You have to take a siesta sometimes. It's not all work and no play. Isn't that what the gringos say?" He roared with laughter. "Take another drink. You'll feel better."

He handed me the bottle. At his urging, I accepted it and took a small sip and didn't choke. I did feel better.

I told him about the visit from the FBI. Thanks to the power of Juarez gossip, he had already heard about it. Word gets around.

"Rest assured, Selena's dad will not let them take you from Mexico," he said.

"The FBI said if I renounce my citizenship with a warrant waiting for me, it's over. I can never go back."

"That's not true. Once things cool off, you can go back and forth. Who will know the difference? If I spoke English like you, I'd cross over all the time just by saying 'American citizen' at the border, and nobody would stop me."

"But if they stopped me for any reason and ran a check, I'd be arrested for being AWOL from the Navy, plus then I'll also be an illegal alien."

Pancho shrugged.

"Why would you want to go back anyway? When you tire of Juarez, there's all of Mexico to explore to find a new place to live. And you have Selena. What else could you want?"

Of course, his words made me think of everything I could never go back to. I pictured all of Los Angeles. I pictured Douglas, Arizona. I even pictured El Paso. I pictured all the girls I'd known in Los Angeles. I pictured home, with my mom, Leonard, my baby sister Mary. A wave of homesickness hit. A tidal wave, really, but I didn't let on. I didn't think Pancho would understand. His sympathies lay with Selena.

"Peace of mind, I guess," I said. "I can't have that if there's an outstanding warrant waiting for me the day I get checked at the border. And what about seeing my mother?"

Pancho scratched one ear.

"I didn't think about that." He shook his head. His hand caressed the liquor bottle like it was a pet. "Whatever happens next, it's your decision."

"That is the problem, exactly."

We continued drinking.

He started talking about how he planned to build a better spray area so that dust wouldn't get on the cars. His ideas for upgrading the space were interesting. I paid close attention to the technical aspects and offered up some ideas of my own. At some point, we quit talking and started working on it.

We ran a hose along the ceiling just outside the perimeter of the spray booth. Through holes we made in the hose, a fine, even spray of water kept dust from flying into the spray booth area. If it worked the way we thought it would, nothing would come in or out to mess up the paint job he had just finished.

"Get an exhaust fan on the roof. It will be a breeze to install," I said.

Chapter 16
Hangovers Are Not Fun

I woke up in bed. It was morning. Selena was standing over me. She was smiling and fresh. I felt terrible. I had a splitting headache and had no idea how I'd made it back home. The last thing I recalled was working on the paint booth.

Selena kissed me gently. Pain ground all the gears in my brain. I closed my eyes.

"I'm dying."

"You had too much to drink."

"That is a very true statement," I agreed, forcing my eyes open. The world spun wildly. I shut them again. Selena sat next to me and laughed at my misery. Even the freshness of her untroubled voice hurt me.

"Sorry," she said. "Did you know that you don't get mean when you drink? You're very funny and happy."

I groaned.

"Great. How did I get here? I can't remember getting home."

Selena laughed harder.

"Pancho carried you over his shoulder. He was so drunk he was weaving all over the street with me following behind. I couldn't talk him into putting you down. We must have been a sight."

I pictured the night crowd in the plaza staring at Pancho staggering along. This was gossip that wasn't going away any time soon, but the more I pictured it, the more absurd it seemed, me hanging over Pancho's shoulder, and Selena, being her bossy self, trailing behind trying and failing to direct Pancho the same way Aunt Carmen did.

Despite the splitting headache, I laughed until tears rolled down my cheeks. Selena laughed with me. The hangover agony was forgotten for a moment when Selena fell into the bed with me.

"You think that's funny? In the middle of the night, you got up and walked to the bathroom, marched up to the toilet, and peed all over everything like you were watering the garden!"

She was giggling so hard that it took a few moments before she could finish.

"I came up behind you and took your thing in my hand. You acted like I wasn't even there. You put your hands on your hips and let me do the work. Then you turned around and walked past me to the bed and collapsed."

She laughed so hard I could hardly understand her. "I knew sleepwalking is a thing, but I didn't know about sleep-peeing."

Hangover or not, our laughter was good medicine. Selena's presence made me hard. Soon we were rollicking about the bed, our bodies pounding together. Sex is not, apparently, a hangover cure. It just delayed the suffering. I felt sick again afterward, and just lay there. Selena took a shower and went out to work.

After a while, I managed to get up. I showered till I felt a little better, dressed, and walked into the parlor to find Selena and Pancho sitting at a table, empty plates in front of them. Pancho looked the same as ever as if he had not been drunk at all the night before.

I put my hand to my head.

"How are you okay?" I asked Pancho.

He'd drunk much more than I did. He had been drunk when I'd first gotten there, more than matched me drink for drink the whole time I was there, and according to Selena, kept drinking while he was carrying me home.

"He's immune to alcohol," Selena said.

"Someday you will be too," Pancho said. "But come on, Keno, I brought you food that will make you get well pronto. It's get-well food."

Hunger was the last thing on my mind, but I obediently sat down and spooned in as much of the bowl of menudo that I could stomach. It wasn't that much, but I could not refuse. I did refuse the beer that Pancho insisted I drink. Hair of the dog that bit you, my ass.

The food did make me feel better. Especially the tortillas that Selena buttered and fed me. A bowl of 'seven mares' also helped, although I picked out every piece of octopus and dropped it into a bowl in front of Pancho, who ate it as he inhaled another two beers. I finished off guacamole, tacos, a tamale, and two Chile rellenos.

"You should top all that off with a beer," Pancho said.

I shook my head. "Just a pitcher of cold water."

Pancho looked disgusted as he stood up. "You'll get all rusty inside!"

"Uncle Pancho, stop that."

"I take the hint," he said. "I will be on my way. There's nothing to look forward to here, sitting with a man who drinks water!"

He kissed Selena on the cheek and left.

"He's my favorite in the whole family," Selena confided. She stood too.

"We have to get back to work. There's not much help today and look how busy we are already."

Behind the counter, we took over, making up the orders.

Selena put together a Keno Special. Each time she scooped ice cream from a container, she stole a kiss.

"Let's go back to the bedroom," I whispered.

She looked at the customers waiting at the counter.

"What will all these people think?"

"That I love you. That's all."

She giggled, put down the ice cream scoop, wrapped her arms around my neck, and gave me a big kiss. Some of the patrons applauded. Some laughed.

"Now back to work, Kenito de mi Vida."

By the time we got rid of the backlog, a whole new crowd had come inside. Four hours passed before we could snatch a break. I led her into the back room, my head spinning from work with a remaining dash of hangover.

I collapsed, sitting on the side of the bed, holding my head in my hands.

"The room is still spinning," I moaned. "How long is this going to last?"

"I have the perfect solution for that," she said, ripping off her clothes.

"Hurry!" I faked another moan. "I'm dying!"

The hangover was soon overpowered by Selena's solution. It was magic.

Chapter 17
Selena's Shopping

Night in our bedroom was pretty dark and quiet, except for the hum of the air conditioning. The buzz of the alarm on Selena's side of the bed had awakened me. I felt her roll away to turn it off.

"Don't go," I said. It was still dark. I reached out and pulled Selena back down on the bed, urging her not to rush off.

"Postpone the trip for another day."

I rolled, taking her with me. I was flat on my back, and she was astride. I tickled her a little, and she giggled. The light from the clock radio highlighted the edges of her curves, her cheeks, her body, the shadows coloring her mysterious exotic. She wiggled a little and looked toward the door to the ice cream parlor.

"We are running short of everything," she said. Then she

dropped the topic, and we got enthusiastically busy under the covers.

We made love. I thought the topic had been dealt with and put away for another day. She headed for the shower, dried off, dressed in the dark in our room, and tenderly kissed me goodbye.

"Be a good boy and behave yourself."

"You too," I said.

Each time Selena drove to El Paso weekly to shop for ice cream supplies on the US side of the border, I thought about how circumstances had conspired so I could not go with her. It was unavoidable because we required a steady influx of things like ice cream cones, marmalade, chocolate syrup, and the latest 45 rpm rock 'n roll records for the jukebox. The trip was essential, but I was always envious when she prepared to leave. It was painful that I couldn't cross the border.

Normally, she went with Luna, and she often had a pickup following to bring back the big stuff. I didn't ask if Luna was going this time, just clicked on the lamp, sat up in bed and quietly watched her get ready.

"Want me to buy you anything in El Paso?" Selena asked.

"Surprise me." Then I said, "Get a box of Hershey bars with almonds."

I broke them into pieces and put them in sundaes for myself. Selena was not a chocolate person.

She kissed me before she left.

After showering and getting dressed an hour later, I strolled to Pepe's, a few blocks away, for breakfast. Breakfast isn't my usual thing, but it's Selena's routine, and we do this every morning. While the cleaning ladies tidied up the ice cream parlor, we headed out to eat. Today, I was alone. Chilaquiles are my go-to choice, so I requested no eggs from the waitress. Despite that, the eggs arrived, but I tactfully removed them and placed them on the waitress's plate. It seemed she knew I don't eat eggs and took them for herself. I didn't mind at all.

Vania, the waitress, is 25 years old with brown eyes and fair skin. She has short hair and is dressed in a white uniform consisting of a short skirt and a cropped shirt that reveals her belly button. She is wearing white tennis shoes and has a nice smile. Selena likes her to wait on us. "Keno, thank you for the eggs," she giggled, taking my money to settle the bill.

"No thanks needed, Vania. I wish they would put the eggs on a different plate so they don't sit on my chilaquiles."

"You certainly don't like eggs, Keno. Okay, I'll see what I can do when you order again."

I handed her a ten-peso tip. "Keno, thank you. I'd kiss you if Selena would let me."

"Selena's not here," I said with a chuckle. The place was filling up with hungry people.

Vania was a cutie. She came around the counter and planted a kiss on my lips. "Gracias for the eggs and the tip."

Chapter 18
Selena's Secret

The parlor was bustling, so much so that I didn't even notice when Luna entered. She sat at the end of the counter, the farthest point from where I was working. Luna was hard to miss. If you closed your eyes and listened to her conversation, it would be hard to imagine that an eighteen-year-old was speaking. Selena always said that no one in the family knew where her material came from, and everything was dirty. I once suggested she write a book of dirty jokes. She was charming and had a fantastic sense of humor. She was known for bringing the most serious person to fits of laughter. I don't believe the jokes would be as funny if translated into English.

Luna was Selena's favorite sister and had become my favorite, too. Her family was conservative and old-fashioned, especially her father, who always wore a depressingly austere expression, but even he was an easy mark for her.

I often heard her mother scold her for the profanity she used, reminding her that she was a lady. Each time, I heard Luna make a funny joke about her mother, asking her to tone down her dirty mouth.

When Selena and I would visit her family, Luna was the first to greet us. She would kiss Selena, then throw her arms around me and devour me with kisses, cooing, "Kenito, Kenito de mi vida!" She would even sit on my lap while everyone watched and whispered dirty jokes in my ear. When the others grew silent, she said, "This is a private joke!"

Her behavior made me uneasy, but I stopped worrying since it didn't bother Selena or her parents. It was just Luna's particular form of sisterly affection. All of Selena's other sisters were rather quiet and shy in a way, but Luna made up the difference. She was a genuine charmer, flirtatious, and irresistible. Because of her, I looked forward to our visits with the family. After we opened Keno, Luna came over daily for ice cream and to chit-chat with Selena, mostly about their sisters. I was never part of those conversations, but I often overheard them. No question, Luna and Selena were tight.

Before I saw Luna at the counter, I noticed her tiny car, a new Fiat, parked out front. It had been a birthday present for her eighteenth birthday, Mexico's driving age.

Luna was alone. As I walked towards her, her face lit up mischievously.

[1]"Hola, Kenito! Ven aquí y déjame tocar."

Her voice had a slightly hoarse tone. It was totally sexy. It was loud enough to make me blush. I waved to Nacho to take over.

Sitting beside her, I leaned over and kissed her ever so lightly on her lips.

"How long have you been here?"

She smiled. "I thought you were ignoring me."

"You know I wouldn't do that. I didn't see you."

"I'm not sure I believe you." The smile again.

When she received the coke, she slid it back towards Nacho. "Thank you. I don't want a coke. I would like an ice cream with just a little chocolate syrup."

"You got it. Nacho will get it for you."

In record time, Nacho was back with a sundae.

Luna made a cute face. "That's not enough chocolate."

Nacho smiled back and walked the distance to get more chocolate syrup. It took two additional attempts for her to smile widely and say, "Perfect, Nacho, thank you."

Nacho made a short bow, holding a big smile, and retreated.

---

1. "Hi Kenito! Come over here and let me touch it!"

I was laughing as she started spooning the beautiful treat.

"Want some?"

"Enjoy," I said. "Are you sure you have enough chocolate?"

She showed me a smile between spoon dips.

"I see you didn't go with Selena to El Paso."

"She left early," she said, still dipping in the ice cream. "Not the regular time."

"She had at least four stops to do, one of them the record store," I told Luna.

She finished the ice cream, put down the spoon, and reached into her purse for a cigarette. "I always tag along with her, but today, she didn't want me to go with her."

I looked at her for a moment. There was an unaccustomed furrow across her brow, and she seemed to avoid direct eye contact. Her bubbly self disappeared, and now she appeared troubled. "Why wouldn't she want you to go along?"

"I'll tell you in a minute," she inhaled the smoke into her lungs.

"Is something wrong, Luna?"

She took a deep drag of the cigarette. [2]"He estado

---

2. I've been playing it cool so far but I need to talk to you in private.

actuando con calma hasta ahora, pero necesito hablar contigo en privado."

Her eyes were full of tears. I couldn't imagine what was going on. This was not like Luna.

"Let's go to the back," I said, already up.

She nodded soberly and slipped off the stool.

The jukebox had not stopped playing.

She left her cigarette in the ashtray and blotted her eyes with a napkin.

As we entered the bedroom, a mixture of smells enveloped the room, blending with the noise from the jukebox that dimmed as I closed the door for quiet, and Luna went into my arms. Now she was really crying hard.

"Tell me, what is wrong, Luna? What is it?"

"Give me a moment; this will pass," she hugged me tight.

I broke away and reached for a box of Kleenex on the nightstand and I handed it to her as she sat on the edge of the bed. I pulled the bedside chair in front of her and sat down.

Her eyes were red, but the tears subsided. "My sister will never forgive me for telling you."

"Nonsense, your sister loves you."

"She will hate me."

I made no comment. Talking was delaying what she wanted to say.

During the pause, Luna said, "Be patient; I need to figure out how to do this."

"Do what?"

"Please be patient."

How wonderful it would be if this were a drama-filled way to tell me a joke. But that's not what was happening. I tried to be patient. She reached for my hands, and I slid on the cushioned chair to reach both her hands.

She released my hands, reached for her purse next to her on the bed, and took a cigarette from the package. "Light me up, I'm going to tell you." She extended her cigarette, and I lit it for her with the lighter I carried in my pocket. I didn't smoke, but everyone else did and never had a match. Selena kept an ashtray on the nightstand. She didn't smoke either, but it was made of onyx and was really a pretty decorative piece.

"Selena is cheating on you with her old boyfriend, Sergio," Luna said, taking a deep breath. "There, I said it. I love my sister very much, but I heard the FBI and Federales came to see you and gave you 30 days, or they would be back for you." She sighed. "I had to tell you what I know."

I was enveloped in a storm of emotions. Betrayal pierced my heart, disbelief clouded my mind, and the weight of broken trust anchored my soul. In that moment, I found myself grappling with the shattered fragments of my world, desperately seeking understanding and solace, and a whirlwind of confusion and anguish gripped my every thought.

"Thank you," I said, trying to control my teeth from chattering. "I need to know everything."

"Sit next to me." She patted the edge of the unmade bed where she was sitting. I rose from the chair and joined her. We both had to look sideways to see each other. "You're trembling," she observed.

"I got chills all of a sudden. I need to know the details. Please."

Luna grasped my hand, sighed, and began. "Months ago, we ran into Sergio when we were shopping for the ice cream shop. It was an accident. He just happened to be in El Paso and took us to lunch. He was a perfect gentleman and treated Selena like an old friend. That was it. Then the next week, while we were shopping. She said we should hurry because we were going to have lunch with Sergio again."

Luna turned her face away and stopped talking.

"Luna, tell me."

At least a full minute of silence before Luna began to speak.

"What if George finds out?" I said to Selena.

"We're not going to tell George. Besides, it's just lunch."

I stopped being negative, and we went to lunch with him.

"Three days later, you needed supplies again. I was here when she told you it couldn't wait."

"I don't remember," I said.

"She told me I couldn't go with her. She said she was meeting him at the Rialto in downtown Juarez and then going to El Paso for the shopping."

"Is Rialto a hotel?"

"Yes. Should I stop?"

"No, don't stop."

Pain gripped my heart. Selena had always been affectionate and loving. How could she be unfaithful? How could she appear so open and caring with me while hiding this other side? We had made love that morning. The bitterness in my throat mounted. Anger, dizziness, and sickness overwhelmed me. If I was sharing Selena with another man, why was I sacrificing everything to be in Juarez, Mexico?

"Wait, Luna, I have to run to the bathroom. Sorry."

I retched up everything I'd eaten that morning. After purging, I washed my face, brushed my teeth, gargled with Listerine, and returned to the bedroom.

"Kenito, you're white. Are you okay?" Luna rose quickly, as if ready to catch me if I stumbled. We embraced, and I held her close.

"I love you, Luna. I'm sorry if this puts you in a difficult spot with your sister."

"I'm sorry too." She hugged me tighter. "I don't want you to close the door on the United States and the thirty days are running out."

At that point, I didn't know if Selena had sex with Sergio at the Rialto, but I was certain she had. I doubted they went to a hotel just for lunch. Was Selena seeing her old boyfriend or was she cheating like Luna said? I was baffled.

"I need to sit," I said. I settled into the bedside chair, and Luna sat on my lap, her arms around me. Her scent was a total turn-on, but how could I feel that way after being hit with such sad news? But that's how I felt.

"I need to ask - did she tell you if she did it? I know it sounds stupid."

"They did it. The Rialto was their regular spot before she went to my aunt in Los Angeles." Sigh. "I sound mean. I'm sorry. I feel like you need to know. I don't want to be mean." Luna teared up again. I felt her tears on my shoulder. She hugged me tighter. We were silent.

Luna sniffed. "Have you noticed a difference in her lately?"

"We had sex this morning before she got ready; the sun wasn't even out yet."

"She's told me how good sex is between you."

"You guys talk about that?"

"Of course."

"Did she tell you how good sex is with Sergio?"

Silence.

"Yes. In the past. Before you came along. When they were dating. We tell each other everything. Always have."

"I think she's always loved this guy, but she said it was over."

Maybe she liked to have two flames going at a time. I knew so little about her. Everything between Selena and me had happened so fast. I pushed the marriage thing, thinking it was a way to keep us together. Fucking fool, I am. Selena wasn't anxious at all about getting married. Maybe this was the reason. But she said yes. She said yes.

"I'm sorry." She whispered in my ear. No longer crying. Still on my lap. Much like when she told me jokes in my ear when we visited her parent's house. Without warning, she whispered. "I feel a bat pressing my [3]culo. Let's get on the bed."

"Luna, get serious."

"I'm serious." She got off my lap and sat facing me on the edge of the bed. Luna dropped the bed talk and said, "I told Selena to break up with you if she wanted Sergio that bad. People get divorced all the time!"

"What did she say?"

"She told me to mind my own business."

---

3. Ass

"Yesterday, I told her if she went to El Paso today without me, then I'd know she was meeting up with him, and I'd tell you."

"What did she say?"

"She said she didn't believe I'd do that to her."

Luna's eyes were red.

When calm was back, I got up and headed for the door.

"Where are you going?"

"I need to get something to drink. Want a coke?"

"Yeah, a coke," she said. "What are you getting?"

"Same," I said.

I wanted a beer or Presidente. I could use a big dose of numbness at that moment, but I resisted. I got us a couple of cold bottles. When I returned, Luna was propped against the headboard with two pillows. Her shoes were off. Her clothes were on. I handed her the Coke, and she took a sip and placed it on the nightstand next to the ashtray. I gulped mine down in record time.

"Sit here with me," she said. "Want to see me naked?"

"Luna, stop with the jokes. Dirty stuff like Selena is doing."

"This won't be dirty," she said. "I promise." Just a little while ago, she was crying, and now it was a giggle.

"Not dirty but wrong."

She took a drink of the soda. I sat on the chair facing the bed.

"Chicken," she said in English. A giggle.

"Let me ask you something," I said, ignoring the chicken remark.

"Ask me anything."

"Your dad and mother were devastated when Selena slept with Sergio. I mean, I understand them being upset, but why so upset they sent her away?"

"Because she stayed out all night. They were fucking all the time, but that was okay because no one knew it. The sin was staying out all night with a man who is not your husband. A bad influence supposedly for all our sisters who haven't fucked yet."

"I want to laugh," I said.

"Laugh, Kenito."

I didn't laugh. Luna shrugged. "Kick your shoes off and sit next to me over here." She patted a spot on the bed.

I was tired to my bones. The news about Selena had wiped me out. Her actions dragged my emotions on a roller coaster. I stepped out of my loafers. Luna made room for me on some of the pillows.

"More like it, Amorcito," she said.

Pillows were against my back and the bed beneath the

rest of me. Luna was to my side, our heads turned to face each other.

"Luna, you talk dirty and tell the best jokes I have ever heard. I mean, the best. But I think you're innocent. That's the wrong word. I don't believe you have been with a man. I believe you're a virgin. Tell me the truth. I'm curious."

In a split second, she straddled me. Her eyes were penetrating, inches from my face. At least the only thing I had taken off was my shoes.

"I'm not a virgin," she said. "Fuck me, and you'll see no blood."

"Luna, that's disgusting." I made a face.

She laughed.

"I suppose the reason you weren't thrown out of the house is that you didn't spend the night out. That's the difference?"

"I wouldn't stay out all night. It would be disrespectful. It's my parents' house, not mine."

I was still sitting up on the bed, and she was sitting across from me, on crisscrossed legs.

"You should become a lawyer," I said. "You have a gift with that mouth."

"Want to see what my mouth can do to this?" she said, grabbing me there. "Hey, what happened? It was so hard a little while ago. Did I turn you off?"

"You didn't turn me off," I said.

"I have Presidente," I said. "Do you want a shot?"

"Si. Si."

I got up to retrieve an open bottle from the storage room.

"I'll get you a glass," I said.

"No need. Bring it here."

I handed it over, passed the chair, and returned to where I had been on the bed before I offered her the bottle. She tilted her head up and the bottle back, and I saw bubbles of air shoot through the glass and the level drop as she swallowed. She did not flinch.

I did. I winced as she chugged it down like it was sweet tea.

The first time Pancho gave me a shot, it nearly took off my head.

"Best brandy there is," she said like an expert would.

"I didn't even know it was brandy," I confessed.

She giggled. "It was dedicated or something for President Adolfo Lopez Mateo only a couple of years ago. My Uncle Pancho loves it."

"I know he does," I said with a chuckle.

"And he carried you home from his shop when you got drunk on it." She giggled again after saying that.

"I wasn't that drunk. I was tired."

I heard myself laugh, and I hadn't even had a drink yet.

She handed me the bottle. I took a slow drink and swallowed carefully. It burned all the way down, but not in a painful way. I could almost feel the numbness and comfort already. I put the bottle down on the table Pancho had built, and after a while, I took another long pull. The Presidente washed more bitterness from my head and warmed my insides.

Nothing Selena said or did would persuade me to take her back. I had already made up my mind. All the promises in the world wouldn't make me change my decision. The hurt was too great. My trust in her, maybe in all women, was destroyed. My fairytale princess was a tramp.

I leaned forward, held Luna's face with my hands, and kissed her full on the mouth.

"We're not doing this," I said. My hands were on her face, just as hers were on mine. Our eyes were maybe three inches apart.

"As you wish," she said. Her smile was fucking beautiful.

I yawned.

The liquor was a sleeping potion.

Chapter 19
The End Of Us

When we woke, we were lying down, facing each other, her hands on me and my hands on her. Took a second to realize why we woke up and who I was looking at.

Selena was back, a Selena I had never seen before, wearing an expression I could neither identify nor describe. Selena was frozen. Shock, horror, or some other emotion distorted her features as she gawked. Luna looked over her shoulder. We all stared at one another.

I'll never forget the look on Selena's face.

"Don't worry. I couldn't get him to fuck me."

"Fucking tramp. Just like your mother."

"Okay, my mother is my excuse. What's yours? Who is the tramp here?"

I sat up. They were arguing around me like I wasn't there.

And the argument lost me. They were sisters, so they made no sense.

"He knows everything," Luna said. "You left me no choice."

"I thought we were a lifelong package," I said, staring up at Selena.

"Wasn't it you that told me that nothing is forever?"

"No, it wasn't me," I said.

Everything was moving in slow motion.

Selena's mouth moved for several seconds before a sound came out.

"After this, we can never make it," Selena said.

"After what, fool?" Luna shouted. "We didn't do anything."

"We're finished, George."

She turned her back on us and walked out.

Her words hit me like weapons, even though I'd have said something similar. My numbness was shattered again. The confusion, hurt, and exhaustion were too great to bear. I could not respond.

I lay still. Selena left. Luna jumped from the bed, fully clothed, as soon as the door was closed. We were both fully clothed.

"What was that about, Luna? You're sisters-"

"Want to know another secret Selena never told you?"

"Is it another bullet? I can't take another bullet."

"It's not about Selena. It's about me. My parents aren't my parents."

"I don't get it," I said.

"Selena's mother and father are not my real mother and father."

No wonder Luna didn't look like Selena or any of the sisters. She acted like them, though, especially Selena.

"I had no idea."

"My mother was the family housekeeper. I was a year old when my mother came to be the live-in, but it's not like I remember being anywhere other than there. When I was four, we were crossing the street to visit the bodega, and there was a fast car. She threw me out of the way and was run over. She saved my life. Then they just kept me, like I was one of the daughters."

"I'm sorry, Luna. I'm sorry."

"It's okay. Everyone in the family knows the story. I've always been treated just like my sisters and told that I am one of them. Everything I have, they gave me. They have always been there for me. But sometimes, when I joke around and go too far, I overhear my dad telling my mom that I'm a tramp like my mother was. Maybe that's just dad being dad, but it makes me wonder if, before she was a housekeeper, my mother was something else entirely."

I felt a pang of sympathy as Luna's words hung in the air. I straightened up and hugged her tightly. "I'm sorry, Luna. No one should say that about you. Not your dad. And not Selena."

"How can anyone really know if my real mom was a whore unless they slept with her and paid her? For all I know, my present dad got some from my real mom. Maybe how I speak is like a tramp, but I don't mean it. I'm just being me." Luna's voice cracked, and tears welled up in her eyes.

Chapter 20
Selena Was Truly Gone

Selena had indeed departed from my life. The sheepish look on Nacho's face suggested that he had eavesdropped on the intense dispute between Selena and Luna. By this point, it was probable that everyone was aware that I had secluded myself in the bedroom with Luna for the entire afternoon. Oblivious to Selena's infidelity, I had unknowingly become a fall guy in everyone's perspective.

As I surfaced, I put on an apron. Why was I taken aback? Why hadn't I foreseen her presence there? Regardless, it was an accomplished fact. Selena had left for good, and I had to face this harsh reality. It felt clear to me that my next step had to be leaving for the United States. Without Selena, there was no reason for me to remain in Juarez.

The gravity of this decision hit me as I reentered the ice cream parlor. The lively melodies of The Everly Brothers' "Cathy's Clown" continued to fill the room, masking the previous outbursts of Selena and Luna in a cacophony of sound. As the jukebox played on uninterrupted, it was possible that the customers may have heard the shouts that came before, but amidst the ongoing music, understanding remained elusive.

The persistent tunes muddled any attempts to decipher the earlier commotion, blending past disturbances into the current symphony of noise. I would soon depart.

I worked behind the counter for a few moments. Everyone watched me as if I were a lit fuse ready to explode. I returned to the bedroom. Luna was dressed and seated by the bed, smoking a cigarette. She leaned back in the chair, crossing her legs. I could see the lines from the comb in her damp hair. Her complexion was slightly rosier than in the morning, but the day's events seemed to leave her unfazed.

"The shower is terrible, but the air-conditioning in here feels amazing," she said.

"It has to run day and night," I replied.

"Is she gone?" Luna asked without moving.

"She is. As far as I'm concerned, she's gone forever. Selena can have an amicable divorce. She'll be free, and we'll both be free to do as we please. I don't want your parents to know what caused the split. Promise me you won't say anything. No one needs to know what really happened."

"I know nothing," Luna said.

"That's a promise?"

"I promise."

"I got to figure out my next move," I said.

"They will put you in jail for running away, won't they?"

"Jail, for sure. I'll have to be cautious about returning. If I don't go directly to the Navy, things will get worse for me. I can't risk getting caught between here and San Diego."

"I can't bear the thought of you being in jail!"

"Neither can I." It was a sobering thought, but I laughed.

"Kenito, you laughed!" She hugged me. "Are you feeling better?"

I tightened the hug. "I am. I'm still hoping I'll wake up and realize today was a nightmare."

"Do you want me to go to San Diego with you? I can drive you there and stick around to visit you in jail. I'll tell my parents I want to go to school there."

I chuckled just a little. "You're so sweet."

"I mean it."

I kissed her lightly, then kissed her again. I pulled away.

[1]"Necesitamos comportarnos," I said.

[2]"Como tú digas. Kenito."

---

1. We need to behave.
2. Whatever you say. Kenito.

Luna gestured at the cigarette in her mouth so I could light it.

Chapter 21
The Bravest Woman I Would Ever Know

Unbeknownst to Selena and her parents, I was behind Luna's and Selena's parents' house with Luna. I had changed into fresh jeans and a clean T-shirt, packing the rest of my clothes. Despite the late hour, the air was hot and muggy, causing my t-shirt to be drenched in sweat. Dim streetlights barely penetrated the thick, humid air, and the sounds of nighttime insects filled the sweltering atmosphere.

Luna's Fiat was too small for the task, so I walked to the back of one of Luna's father's cars. (Luna opened the trunk.)

"This is a big risk for you," I said, looking at Luna.

"I told you, I know the agents at the crossing. I always flirt with them, and I've never been subjected to a search. I cross all the time," Luna said.

"We agreed we were doing this and already discussed the possible risk. I want to do this for you."

I gently kissed her. It wasn't long, but how her lips responded made it special.

I peered into the dim space I was about to crawl into. The streetlight didn't illuminate much inside the trunk, and neither did the bulb that flickered on when the trunk opened. The spare tire was gone, but the crowbar and jack remained. The trunk was surprisingly clean for a frequently used vehicle. As I lay down, I heard the crunch of dried leaves, similar to what you might sweep from a seldom-used hallway, but it didn't concern me. Although it was cramped, I found a relatively comfortable position. However, it smelled unpleasant - a mix of car exhaust, oil, gasoline, and cigarettes.

"It's going to get hot in there," she warned.

"I'm more worried about you. I'm sorry I got you into this."

"Kenito, stop. I want to do this. Get in there." She gave me a lightweight shove and giggled.

I lay there rigidly, feeling every divot in the road, listening to every bump, bounce, squeal, and vibration from the street. My watch ticked slowly. El Paso was close. I knew we weren't going far, but time dragged slowly. I thought how terrible it would be for Luna if we got caught. For my part, I was going to jail anyway.

I had consumed a lot of brandy and even some beer, and I was feeling queasy. The trunk was exceedingly hot, and I could feel the sweat dampening my jeans. I'm not usually claustrophobic, but the combination of my nerves, the effects of drinking, and the confined space in the car made it incredibly uncomfortable.

I felt the car slow down, stop, and move slowly again. It happened several times. I heard voices talking, but not clearly enough to understand the conversation. I was going crazy with anxiety. The car began to move again. I prayed we had cleared customs at each stop and start, but it's not like the trunk had windows. I could not tell if we were moving forward in a line at customs, traffic in the street, or what else might be happening.

Our journey continued a bit further before we came to a halt. A key turning in the lock sent a chill down my spine as the trunk sprung open. Luna's face appeared above me, framed by the night sky and a wall fragment. We had parked behind a gas station. The realization that we were in Texas filled me with excitement.

"I need to change," I informed Luna, feeling the dampness of my clothes. "I'm all wet."

"Did you wet yourself?" she teased.

"No, I didn't wet myself," I retorted.

[1]"Simplemente estoy bromeando contigo, George." She chuckled.

---

1. I'm just messing with you, George.

I gave her a rapid kiss. "I know you're kidding." Laughing.

I discarded my soaked t-shirt, jeans, and underwear in the restroom trash, grateful for the spare clothes in my duffel bag. Luna patiently waited in the car. As soon as I slid into the passenger seat and shut the door, I moved closer to her. Our embrace felt like a predestined moment. "Thank you," I whispered. "You are the bravest woman I will ever know. Thank you, Luna." Our kiss seemed to stretch on forever.

During that sweltering Texas summer night, the car windows were left ajar, allowing the sultry air to circulate as we engaged in our intimate encounter. My jeans were the first to be shed, quickly followed by my underwear. Her shoes were next, tumbling onto the car floor, followed by her panties. The confined space, coupled with the heat of the night, only amplified the sensuality and eroticism of the moment. Despite fifteen minutes of passionate engagement, I found myself unable to reach a climax. What began as a wild, frenzied encounter gradually transformed into a slow, deliberate dance of desire.

In the aftermath, we clumsily put our clothes back on. "I'm just relieved the FBI didn't stumble upon us in that state," I quipped, a chuckle escaping my lips.

"You're going to make it to San Diego. It's not as if you're El Capone with wanted posters plastered all over town," she retorted, her laughter echoing mine.

"May your words reach God's ears."

"Our next destination is the train station," she declared, her eyes twinkling with mischief. "Why are you sitting all the way over there?" She gestured, a playful smile dancing on her lips. "We just made love. Get over here!"

I slid back next to her, our bodies again in close proximity.

Perhaps I should have alerted the FBI agents in El Paso earlier, but that ship had sailed. The only train bound for California that night was headed to Los Angeles. I blended into the crowd effortlessly, appearing like an ordinary student with nothing but a duffle bag - precisely the image I intended to project. My once neatly trimmed navy hair was now a distant memory. We found a bench and settled down to wait for the train. Luna procured a bag of peanuts from a nearby vending machine, and we idly picked at it while waiting for my journey to begin.

"What about the ice cream parlor and all your money in the bank?" Luna asked.

"There's not that much in the bank. We paid Carmen off. Thank God for that. Selena can have whatever is there and do whatever she wants with the store."

"The store was a hit. People are going to miss it. Especially the jukebox."

"Maybe Selena and Sergio can take over," I mocked.

"It won't happen. He has two bars, big saloons loaded with pool tables."

"Good for him."

"Let's not talk about my sister or him." She snuggled up close. Her short skirt high on her thighs.

"I came here with nothing, and I'm leaving the same way. The only thing I lost was a wife that I never really had. But I've gained friends, so it hasn't been a total loss."

At one-thirty in the morning, the passenger loading of the train to Los Angeles was broadcast over the loudspeaker. It was time for goodbye. We walked over to the gate and waited for it to open. Luna's eyes were shining with tears. She hugged me tightly.

"I'm not good at goodbyes," I said. The hug became a kiss, then another kiss.

When the gate opened, I walked through, not looking back. I wouldn't have seen her very clearly through the tears. With each step toward the platform, the inevitability of fate weighed heavier on me. I wiped my eyes. A few deep breaths and squaring my shoulders did not muster up the courage I was looking for.

Chapter 22

Train Ride

The heat in El Paso was scorching, while the train's cold felt icy. As I boarded, I received a small pillow and blanket. Despite the chilling cold, I opted to keep the blanket for later use. Rifling through my duffel bag, I retrieved a jacket that had been with me in Mexico City during my time with Selena after our wedding. The memories of that chilly period flooded back. As the train embarked on its journey, anticipation coursed through me. Thoughts of the future overwhelmed my mind, and a sense of panic gripped my stomach. With each passing minute on American soil, the risk of arrest loomed larger. The consequences would be dire if the police or the FBI apprehended me. Having crossed the border hidden in the trunk of a car to evade detection, I now found myself in plain sight on a train bound for Los Angeles.

The train would halt to let off and take on passengers at each town we passed, and each stop only heightened my anxiety. Have you ever tried to evade them? You wouldn't believe how many police officers are around. About two hours after departing from the El Paso Station, I was a nervous wreck.

An unexpected distraction saved me from the paranoia and the apex of my anxiety.

No one was immediately behind, in front of my seat, or across the aisle. The only lights on in my coach were at the exits. The two seats I was occupying weren't wide enough for me to lie down, but I managed to curl up with the blanket on me. The train stopped, and I was jolted awake as passengers exited or came aboard. I kept trying to sleep.

"Can I share this seat with you?" A hand tapped my leg.

I squinted my eyes toward the girl who was speaking. I barely saw her in the dark. I made out that she was wrapped in a blanket but didn't see much else. At the last stop, there had been at least fifty empty seats in this coach, but explaining that would have taken more consciousness than I had at that moment. I moved into the window seat, giving her the aisle.

"Sit," I said, shutting my eyes and trying to coil into position.

She leaned over towards me and spoke in a low voice. "I've been sitting toward the back. I saw you earlier when you went to the john, and I know you aren't a bad guy. I'm the only girl traveling alone in this car. There are seven men spread out."

I turned to look at her and managed to open my eyes. She was close to my age and cute.

"Yeah, I'm a good guy," I said. "My name is George." As soon as I opened my mouth, the anxiety struck again. What if she was a cop? Why did I give her my name?

"My name is Zoe," the girl said. "Where are you going?"

"LA," I replied.

"Me too."

A few seconds passed. I tried again to get comfortable, but I needed that second seat. And Zoe didn't look any more comfortable than I was.

"Zoe, if you want to lie on the seats across the aisle, I'll look out for you. I promise no one will bother you. And that way, we can both stretch out a little."

"Good idea," she said.

I heard rustling, and when I opened my eyes again, I could make out her sitting down and lowering her shade. I realized mine was open, and I closed it.

She waved, and I waved back. I shut my eyes and was out like a light.

Awakening to a sudden chill on my left bicep, I found Zoe's icy hand had found its way up my coat sleeve.

"Would it be alright if I stay here?" she asked, her voice a whisper in the cold air. She had already nestled herself into the narrow space next to me, her body pressed against mine, her hand still gripping my arm.

"Of course," I responded.

"Thank you. The air conditioning has been on full blast since we boarded," she murmured, her words barely audible over the hum of the train. "I can't believe how cold it is."

"It is cold," I agreed, closing my eyes and allowing my mind to wander back to the enchanting image of Luna.

In time, I became aware of her allure - a beautiful stranger with a scent reminiscent of Selena, yet her curls were uniquely Zoe's. My thoughts drifted from my wife to Luna, a secret smile playing on my lips.

"Let me adjust our blankets," she offered.

As she rose, I felt the cold air rush in to fill the space she had occupied. Her hip brushed against mine as she gathered my blanket, and then she skillfully draped both our blankets over me before sliding back into her spot. Her hands were icy as they closed around mine, and she rested her head on my chest, just below my shoulder.

"Thank you, George," she murmured.

"Anytime," I replied.

In the hushed darkness of the train coach, a clandestine dance unfolded. Our hands, once strangers, began to explore unfamiliar territories. Slipping under her coat, my fingers traced the curve of her waist, eventually finding the warmth of her skin. Simultaneously, her hand mirrored my actions, exploring my form under darkness. Our secret was safe beneath the two blankets, shielding us from the biting cold.

I drifted back into a light slumber, only to be roused when the train stopped. I remained motionless, lying on my right side, my head cushioned by the pillow. My legs were curled up, my stocking-clad feet pressing against the armrest of the aisle seat near Zoe's feet. Our faces were mere inches apart, our legs entwined in a silent ballet. The blankets draped over us, concealing our intertwined forms from the world brought a sense of uncertainity.

The fear of her revealing a badge had dissipated, replaced by a comforting sense of intimacy. I found solace in the soft breath of a stranger on my face and the warmth of her body against mine. Despite our coats, there was a shared warmth, a connection I hadn't realized I needed until that moment.

"Are you okay?" she asked.

"I'm fine. You?"

She kissed me.

"Thank you," she spoke in my mouth.

* * *

With its numerous stops, the train trip from El Paso to Los Angeles spanned eighteen hours. As dawn broke, the sun's rays pierced through the unshaded windows, rousing me from my slumber and bathing the coach in a warm glow. Zoe, too, stirred awake. The coach was still very cold.

"You're stunning," I murmured, conscious of my morning breath.

"I dig your curly hair," she said, gently pulling. (I was reminded of Luna just hours ago when we did it in her father's car. Only Luna didn't pull gently.)

"You have great curls, too," I said, softly touching them."

Zoe was the first to rise, stretching in the aisle. I followed suit. We had slept in our coats and socks, our shoes discarded on the floor by our seats. As we made our way to the restrooms at the back, I noticed four passengers still cocooned in their blankets, presumably asleep.

Upon returning to our seats, we slipped on our shoes and headed for the dining room. My clothes were packed in my duffle bag, but I lacked toiletries. Fortunately, we stumbled upon a sundry store en route to the dining coach, where I purchased toothpaste, a toothbrush, and mouthwash.

The only thing I remember about that breakfast is the tantalizing aroma of the coffee.

"I'm a twenty-two-year-old divorcee heading to my parent's place in Los Angeles to regroup," Zoe shared. "What about you? Are you on the run too?"

I grinned."Sort of. And thanks for keeping me warm."

"The pleasure was mine," Zoe responded. "How old are you, George?"

I wasn't going to tell her I was four years younger. "About your age," I lied.

After breakfast, we returned to the coach. I brushed my teeth with my new toothbrush. Los Angeles was just three hours away.

"I didn't anticipate the cold on the train, considering how hot it was in El Paso," I remarked.

"I've traveled by train before. It's always chilly. I should've worn a warmer coat," Zoe admitted.

"How long were you married? Or is that too personal?" I asked.

"No more personal than last night," she replied.

She smiled, and I smiled.

"I was married for eighteen months. I should've known being an Army wife wouldn't be easy. I left him three times. He'd come back to LA each time and persuade me to return. Not this time."

We managed to create a snug little haven for ourselves on the seats, our feet tucked under us, wrapped in blankets, facing each other.

"Would you like to snuggle up like we did last night?" Zoe proposed, her teeth chattering in the chilly air. Her smile was warm and inviting, revealing a charming little gap between her two front teeth. She was undeniably attractive, with her large, captivating eyes and bouncy curls.

"Good idea, let's snuggle," I said. "I feel like I've known you for a long time."

"I was about to say the same."

We attempted to recreate the previous night's position, but it didn't last long. We found ourselves in one of the lavatories, succumbing to the moment's spontaneity. There's something about spontaneous intimacy that makes it incredibly thrilling.

When we returned to our seats, we abandoned the blankets. For the remainder of the journey, we sat shoulder to shoulder, her right arm draped around my left, her hand resting on my upper thigh, her head nestled on my shoulder.

Now and then, she would nuzzle my neck, a sweet gesture that made the journey all the more memorable.

We exchanged our parents' numbers. I never confided where I was ultimately headed.

I helped her out with three pieces of luggage. A porter took charge of it when we were off the train. We had become friends. All these years have gone by, and I still remember her.

"My parents will be in the depot," she said. "Are you taking a taxi?"

Agreeing was the easiest thing to do. "Yes," I said. "A taxi."

I hugged her.

Chapter 23
Such a Fool

I didn't opt for a taxi ride. Instead, I found myself in the heart of downtown Los Angeles, the city's pulse echoing in my ears. I strolled from the bustling Union Station, crossing the street to the vibrant Olvera Street, where I indulged in four tantalizing taquitos. The taste brought back memories of Selena and me and our shared meals in the lively city of Juarez.

A taxi ride to my parents' house was out of the question. I knew that my journey to San Diego required a bus or train. So, I roamed the downtown streets, lost in a mental tug-of-war for several hours. I was like a pendulum, swinging between decisions, almost succumbing to the allure of the easy way out. But the thought of the impact my hiding would have on my parents held me back. I couldn't bear to put them through that.

Eventually, I found myself at the Greyhound Depot on 6th & Los Angeles, with memories of my mother and me arriving years ago. A bus to San Diego was my only option. The wait for the next bus was agonizingly long, and when I finally boarded, my nerves were wound tighter than ever.

Each passing mile brought me closer to an impending punishment. The journey is a blur in my memory, but my emotions are etched deep within my heart. The escalating fatigue and fear fueled my imagination, painting vivid and increasingly terrifying scenarios of turning myself in.

Stepping off the bus, I was a bundle of nerves, sweating and trembling—a biting breeze sliced through my damp t-shirt, sending shivers down my spine. I was desperate for a drink, believing it would give me the necessary courage. Oh, the lies we tell ourselves to cope.

By then, it was either too late to get to the Balboa Navy hospital to turn myself in, or that was just something I was telling myself. I was afraid to go to a bar in San Diego. I was underage to drink in a US bar and didn't want to take any chance of getting arrested. My last place of duty was Balboa Navy Hospital, the proper place to surrender.

I took a bus to San Ysidro, right at the Mexican border.

At San Ysidro, I could walk across the border to Tijuana without being questioned. I wasn't sure about returning, but I didn't even think about it. I walked into Mexico—a piece of cake. The risk I had put Luna through to smuggle me across the border, and here I was back in Mexico. I was a fool, no question about it.

I Iook a taxi to town. The tourist section was crowded with people milling about, getting drunk, amusing themselves. The tourist section was too dangerous for me. No one was looking for me in Mexico, but paranoia is a bitch.

I found a bar on the outskirts of the business district. By the time I got there, the crowd was already pretty worked up, and the crazy mood was infectious. I wanted to warm up quickly. In my head, I was calling it celebrating my last night of freedom. I bought a couple of drinks at once and swallowed them both in a few gulps. The comforting burn came up from my toes. I stopped shaking.

"Give the bar a round," I told the bartender.

"Si, señor," he said.

I was used to carrying a lot of cash. Pretty soon, I was buying drinks for the house. I asked the bartender to run a tab for me, and he agreed. The drinks were cheap. I suddenly became very popular.

"Ola," a girl greeted me.

"Ola. Sit and have a drink with us. We're having a party."

The girl leaned forward. Though not as conventionally stunning as Zoe, Selena, or Luna, and certainly not sixteen or seventeen, she had a distinct charm. Her pronounced dark brows added character to her features, and the effects of the evening had taken a toll on her makeup.

In a conversational tone, she propositioned, "You could have a great time with me for less than what you're spending on these leeches, you know."

Politely declining, I responded, "Thank you for the offer, but now I'm seeking a few drinks and some engaging conversation."

She did not fit the image of a classic beauty. You know those country songs about girls becoming more attractive as the night goes on? They're sometimes accurate. Although she did become more captivating as the evening progressed, it wasn't what I was looking for at that moment.

Soon, I was roaring drunk. After the first round, the bartender didn't ask for payment. I didn't realize the tab size until it was too late.

I found ninety dollars in cash when I attempted to settle my bill. The bill was eighty dollars more than that. I asked for a countercheck, but everything hit the fan when the management saw the check was on an account in Juarez.

"You can't write a check, señor. Cash only."

I shook my head and tried to explain in my best Spanish.

"I have a business in Juarez, amigo. The check is good as gold. You'll see if you call the bank. Believe me."

The barman shook his head. His boss shook his head.

"Bank is closed, señor. Everything is closed. And no matter. We accept cash only here."

The bartender and I squared off and argued. I don't know how long it took, but before it was resolved, the police were on the scene.

"Since when are counter checks no good in Mexico?"

I was as boozed up as you might expect and belligerent. Selena had told me that I was not a mean drunk.

"Cash, señor. No checks."

"I always write a check. My check is good, I tell you!"

I was arrested. I was thrown into a concrete room flowing with urine, a room which contained others who might pass, marginally, as human, but you could argue either way- Tijuana jail. I was so far gone I passed out in an alcoholic stupor, which was a blessing. The stupor did not last long enough.

I was roused from sleep by an odor so disgusting it was beyond anything I had ever experienced. No cesspool on earth could rival it. Fortunately, my stomach was already devoid of contents. My olfactory senses were the first to awaken, followed by a throbbing headache. My eyes remained shut, perhaps in refusal to accept reality. Unfortunately, one cannot shut off their hearing. A peculiar sound, a damp, rhythmic friction, filled the air. It was unfamiliar, yet incessant. When I finally mustered the strength to open my eyes and locate the source of the noise, I was met with the sight of bodies scattered across the floor. It was akin to viewing abstract art. Not beautiful, but perplexing. I could not comprehend the scene before me, so I continued to stare, attempting to decipher it.

Two men were sprawled on the damp, grimy floor. It was beyond my understanding. I had no context for what was unfolding in my nearly eighteen years.

Eventually, my brain processed the sight. The image was etched into my memory with brutal precision. I assumed both men had their trousers rolled up to their knees. Then, I noticed the man closer to me was completely devoid of pants, and his legs terminated below the knee. I had seen amputees before but never in such a state of undress. However, it wasn't his lack of legs that was most unsettling. The other man was still, either unconscious or deceased. The legless man was clutching him tightly, his hips moving with fervor. The horrifying realization of what I witnessed hit me like a tidal wave. I shut my eyes, wishing I could do the same with my ears. The disgust was overwhelming.

When I next awoke, I was hesitant to open my eyes. I prayed that the horrific ordeal was over, that I would find myself safe in bed with my beautiful, loving wife in our rooms behind El Keno Ice Cream Parlor. But then, the stench hit me again. I was indeed in a living nightmare.

There were no phones to be found. I was penniless. Without money, meals in a Tijuana jail are non-existent. You subsist on bread and water. So, not only was I in a nightmarish situation, but I was also trapped in it.

In an attempt to overshadow my recollections of Selena, my mind wandered to Luna. I remembered her courage, her stunning beauty, and the memorable encounter we had in the car. My thoughts then shifted to Zoe. I reminisced about how we shared warmth and the intense moment we experienced in the restroom.

Shore Patrol came by the cells early morning to look for military personnel. I still wanted to show up of my own free will and not be found here, so when they came by, I hung back.

The Tijuana jail was hell. The reputation the jail had acquired over decades was terrible, indescribably hellish, and well-deserved. As darkly as it has been painted, I can vouch that anything ever said about it is a gross understatement. In boot camp, we were warned about the jail in Tijuana and to stay clear from crossing the border if we were on leave or stationed in San Diego. They weren't kidding. Regardless of what I was facing, jail in America could not be worse than this. It took five days for me to break my silence.

"Hey, Shore Patrol! Over here. Please!"

The neat-as-a-pin petty officer approached. He looked me up and down, sweaty, dirty, unkempt, stinking of prison and misery. I was a mess.

"I'm Navy. Get me out of here!"

He seemed skeptical. I gave him my ID number.

"Check it out. I'm AWOL. I've been AWOL for months. Ask the FBI. Tell them you have Hatcher. Do whatever you need to, but you get me the hell out of here."

An hour later, the officer was back.

George Hatcher

"Hatcher, you're getting out of here."

I yelled out, "Bravo!"

I had a smile on my face for the first time in ages. I never would have believed I could be so happy to be arrested. But my joy didn't last long.

Chapter 24
Marine Brig

The Shore Patrol escorted me straight to the brig in San Diego. There, I was given prison whites, permitted to shower, shave, and hastily consume what seemed like a decent meal, all under the same pressure as in boot camp. I'd estimate that the brig's cell block is a single level, with less than a hundred cells. The bars are white and spotlessly clean, a stark contrast to my previous surroundings. There was no semblance of privacy. A solid floor beneath, a concrete wall, bars in front and above where guards patrolled and peered down at you. For a few days, I thought it was a definite improvement over Tijuana.

The Navy swiftly brings you to a court-martial for offenses like going AWOL. The type of court-martial you're assigned is the question. There are three types: Summary, Special, or General court-martial. Summary is the least severe, meant for minor incidents. Special court-martial is more severe, where a judge can sentence up to twelve months in the brig, though I don't think that's the maximum. A general court-martial is the gravest level, where the sentence can even be death.

I was aware of these three court types and suspected I might end up in the harshest one, a general court-martial, given that I had fled to Mexico and the FBI was involved. I could see a fiery hell approaching to consume me.

Unlike what you see on TV or in movies, where the accused wears orange jumpsuits in court, the military has a different approach. I was given a set of blues, a full uniform. It wasn't brand new, but it was in near-new condition - you don't appear in court in prison whites.

Two military police officers drove me by jeep to the court on the San Diego base. It was a relief to see something other than bars, to breathe fresh air, and to be out in the open, even though we didn't drive through the city or anything. Everything is located on the base. I was placed in a solitary holding cell. The anticipation was nerve-wracking. The uncertainty of what would happen next was daunting. It's intimidating to be trapped in the gears of justice, a massive machine that processes you grinds you down, swallows you whole, or spits you out.

After a long while, who knows how long, a uniformed officer came to see me. I can still picture him today. He couldn't have been even thirty yet. Though he was a lawyer, he had a boot camp haircut and was clean-shaven and neat in the way only a young military man is. We spoke through the bars. He carried a notepad.

"Hatcher, my name is Roger Hamilton. I'm your lawyer."

"Great to meet you, sir."

He told me I was being charged for being absent without leave.

"You were gone for so long the Navy could have filed a charge of desertion. You are lucky," he said. "The prosecutor is taking your youth into account. You are lucky."

"What does that mean? How much time will I do?"

"First, let me ask you, do you want to plead not guilty or guilty?"

"I'm guilty. Why fool around?"

Roger Hamilton didn't smile, but there was relief in his face that I didn't plan to fight the charge.

"In that case, it is possible we can dispose of your case today. Under an Article 32 hearing, you will be asked to plea to the charges. If you plead not guilty, you are given a date and assigned to one of the three types of court martials. In your case, no doubt it will be a summary or special, but you never know."

"Mr. Hamilton, I just said I will plead guilty."

"I'll try to get the judge in the summary court to accept your plea and pass sentence. Today, the judge is a commissioned officer but not a lawyer. We may get past it all today if we waive and accept his ruling. Sounds like that's what you want."

"Yes."

"You will be given credit for all your time in custody."

"I got it. I want to get rid of this today and start doing whatever time they give me."

"I'll see you in court."

He almost walked away but stood in front of the bars with another question.

"Why did you go to Mexico?"

"I was a fool. I got married. I was floating in a cloud of make-believe."

"If the judge agrees to take your plea and sentence you, he might ask you that question. Come up with a better answer."

"Got it," I said.

The sitting judge agreed to accept my guilty plea and pass the sentence.

"Why did you join the Navy at seventeen, go through boot camp, start corpsman school, then run off for months to Mexico?"

"I have no excuse, your honor."

"If you had an opportunity to return to active duty, would you grab it, or do you want out?"

"I would grab it, your honor."

The judge shook his head. I could not read his expression. Maybe I got a break that he was not a lawyer, a judge who was burned out. He wasn't young, but he wasn't old, maybe forty.

"I am remanding you to the custody of the United States Marines to be held in the brig for one hundred twenty days. I am not ordering a discharge, but you will be stripped of your rank to recruit, and your pay grade will be based on that reduction in rank. Upon completing your sentence, you are ordered to appear at Balboa Naval Hospital to complete the training you started as a corpsman. The time you spent AWOL and time in the brig will extend your four-year term of enlistment."

Without Selena in the picture, I didn't mind returning to the Navy. This time I would stick it out. No running to fucking Mexico or anywhere else. I felt better than I had for a long time. I mean, I wasn't looking forward to being incarcerated for a hundred and twenty days, but now it felt like I had a future.

"Thank you, your honor," my attorney said.

"Thank you, your honor," I said. "Your honor, may I speak?"

"Yes."

"Your honor, my parents must be sick with worry. I don't even know if they know I am back from Mexico. Will you allow me a phone call?"

"So ordered."

George Hatcher

I shook the hand of my attorney, who didn't have much to say. I was returned to the brig, which the Marines operate.

There is no such thing as a phone call in the brig. I got the phone call.

"Mom, I will stay in the Navy after serving the four months. Don't worry about me. Let Dad know I love him, and I love you. I'm sorry I put you through all that I put you through."

You can write one letter per day, but listen to this. They give you a pencil and paper and a stamped envelope. Ten minutes later, they picked up the pencil and envelope. Suppose you are not finished writing, too bad. Try again the next day. You cannot seal the envelopes because mail is censored.

If you get mail, it is delivered to your cell. You have ten minutes to read the letter. Then you must store it or throw it away. No pictures, nothing. You can get visits from family or others by special approval, but there are no visits for the first thirty days. After that, you are allowed one visit per week for one hour. If it's your spouse, you can kiss her on arrival and departure. You cannot hold hands at the visiting table.

I received no visits.

Those four months in the brig were hell. My anxiety increased daily. I could not help remembering everything that had happened. I couldn't do anything about the past and could do nothing but worry about the future. I wrote to my mom and told her I couldn't have visitors. The censor came to tell me I could not lie in a letter. I wrote her another letter telling her that I mentally could not handle a visit, so she should not consider visiting.

I needed to vent. I wanted to write, but the rules were stringent, cruel, and pointless. I managed to squirrel away a pencil and started keeping diary-like notes in the blank spaces of the bible in my cell. It was a small bible, but there was enough space on the top of each page where I could write. It was a huge relief.

"What are you doing?"

A Marine guard making his evening rounds saw me scribbling.

I stood at attention and dropped the Bible on my cot.

Marine guards talk like the drill sergeants you see in movies, with volume at full blast and in your face. In his voice, there's always an abrasive challenge. This guard was generic, average height, buzz cut so short you couldn't tell the color, medium build, voice like an angry foghorn. When he came around, I would have seen him standing there if I hadn't been so wrapped up in writing.

"Writing a note, sir."

"On the Bible? Where did you get the pencil?"

I stood even stiffer.

"I kept a pencil at letter time."

"I'm writing you up. Give that to me!"

I handed over the bible and pencil and was placed in solitary confinement for ten days for defacing a Bible. The cell was dark and cold. The cot where I slept had to be raised at four a.m. and kept that way until taps that evening.

A prisoner could either sit on the concrete floor or pace. Most of the time, I paced.

Every day, I would hear someone scream or cry. It was common for prisoners on solitary row to attempt suicide. It was hard to sneak a razor blade out of the five-minute shower-and-shave break we got each day, but some of the men did.

On my eighth day, my nerves were rebelling. Like other voices I heard sometimes, I was making noise. I should have known better than to draw attention to myself. The door had a small rectangle halfway down that food was shoved through, and above it, a notebook-sized sliding door guarding a face-level window for guards to look through. Otherwise, the door was solid and constructed of an ugly, abused metal stronger than death.

"Come over here!" a guard said through the hatch.

I moved to where he could see me and squinted when the light hit my eyes.

"Yes, sir."

"What are you doing, prisoner?"

"Pacing, sir."

"Pacing. Well, tell you what. Start double-timing in place, and you keep it up until I return and tell you to stop."

"Yes, sir."

Ten minutes later, I was sweating up a storm. I wouldn't say I liked the whole world. I was weak from the crappy food and felt faint. I stopped. Twenty minutes later, after being caught in the act of not double-timing, I wished I hadn't. I was given five more days in solitary confinement and a cell change to a restricted diet location. Not only was I in solitary, but now I was getting war rations for breakfast: a cold potato and cold spinach for lunch and two cold potatoes and spinach for dinner.

I stopped eating altogether. I dumped the potatoes and spinach in the round brass-trimmed hole in the corner of the cell, which served as the toilet. It would've been another violation if they'd learned I hadn't eaten. I would've slashed my wrists if I'd gotten my hands on a razor blade in my cell during those last days. I was so tremendously upset that I came close to cussing every guard that came by. Somehow, I held on. I hated the military. I was sorry I had told the judge I wanted to hang in there. Fuck them.

Chapter 25
Freedom Delayed

On the day of my release from the Brig, I got my wish. Two detectives from Los Angeles were waiting for me in the release area. I was read my rights and handed a copy of what one officer said was a warrant for grand theft. I folded it and put it in my pocket. The first thing I thought about was the drugstore. I was cuffed, hands in front, and I was put in the back of a car.

I was sure I was having a nightmare. I was ready to wake up at any moment.

Once in the car, I managed to get the complaint document the detective had given me. I started reading. I saw Thelma's name as the victim of grand theft. Three counts: one thousand, one thousand, fifteen hundred dollars.

Money taken under false pretense. Grand Theft.

There was no question that I owed her the money. No question that I was a turd to lie to her. There is no question that I was wrong to use fake letters from my father in Arizona. She had every right to be pissed and come after me.

I wondered if life revolves around retribution. Must everyone seek revenge?

It was too late to change the past. I was booked into Los Angeles County Jail, and bail was set.

Bail was impossible. The Navy had a military hold on me. I sat in jail for four more months until my trial. When I arrived, I was put in a cell with two bunks and six other occupants. Five of us were on the cement floor with a blanket. When someone needed to use the toilet, it was an experience never forgotten. After the first month or so, the occupancy level was less; I believe I got a bunk by then.

County Jail was child's play compared to the brig, but I was depressed and miserable.

On a rare day, my public defender came to see me at the jail. I naturally disliked him, his cheap suit, the greasy kid stuff he put on his hair, and the gum he chewed. He was constantly smacking his gum in my face.

"This is a sophisticated crime. Did you do this alone?"

"I don't know what you mean by sophisticated, but yeah, I got the money as a loan. I lied about how I would pay it back. The letters from my dad were phony, but only my dad can say he didn't write them."

"Let's go to trial, and let's bring your dad and let him testify that he wrote you those letters and signed them."

"I just told you they are phony."

"What do you want to do, Hatcher?"

"I want to get this over with. How many more months do I have to be in this jail waiting to get a court hearing?"

"Hatcher, you will get credit for every day you are here. You are doing time. It's not dead time."

"I want to get this over with."

"I will talk to the district attorney and see if we can do a plea bargain and let you cop to one count of grand theft. At your age, with no prior record other than going AWOL, I think the judge will give you probation and maybe make you pay the money back in payments through the probation office. I am not promising you'll get probation. It's up to the judge."

"I understand."

"If you get convicted through trial or a plea, as we are discussing, the Navy will discharge you as an undesirable. Or you will get a general discharge for having been convicted of a felony in a civil court. Are you good with that?"

"I'm good with that," I said. The brig had been an awakening for me. "Make a call and tell them to send me a discharge, and take the fucking hold off me so I can make bail. My parents own a house. They will sign, and I can get out."

"The military doesn't move that fast. Look, it's possible if we try this case, you will win. From what I've seen, this is no dead bang for the prosecutor. I don't understand why the district attorney filed the case. He should have told this victim to sue you for the money."

"I'm guilty. I don't want to fight this. I want to do my time and be free again."

The judge committed me to the California Youth Authority for a period not to exceed three years. He gave me credit for the time I served in the county jail.

Things could have gone easier for me if I had known what I know today. Through its parole board, the Youth Authority could have released me the next day or in a short period. The time depended entirely on my good behavior and the parole board's decision. I could do three years! It didn't ease the pain to know that I had dug my own grave.

I was eighteen. By then, I had served eight months behind bars, four months in the brig, and four months in the county jail. I was making friends behind bars.

I met Mike in the county jail while waiting for trial. He took every opportunity to work out pushups, sit-ups, and dynamic tension. He also took every opportunity to fight. If he wasn't fighting or working out, he was talking about fighting or working out. He would make guys fight him. I listened to many of his stories. We left County on the same day. They sent me to the Deuel Vocational Institute (DVI) in Tracy, California. I didn't know where he went.

DVI, a notorious Youth Authority prison in California, was known for its rough conditions and high population of gang members. Despite its reputation, I was so beaten down that I didn't care where they sent me. DVI wasn't just a facility for juveniles; it also housed adults and was infamous for being a gladiator school. Additionally, my conviction led to an immediate Undesirable Discharge from the Navy due to the civil criminal conviction. Although I had the option to appeal the discharge, which could have potentially resulted in a modified general discharge (considered better than undesirable), I chose not to appeal.

At DVI, I was locked up for several weeks. The housing board determined I was a candidate to have my own room, a cell, but there were no bars. I was given a key to lock my room when I was out, and I locked myself in when it was time to shut down. I was free. Not really free. Not the kind of free like on the outside. On the outside, you don't have to contend with gun towers. I forget how many gun towers there were. Still, on a scale of one to ten, DVI was a ten compared to the fucking brig.

We could open our doors at six in the morning. The mess hall served breakfast, and the yard was available for walking, jogging, or relaxation unless you had work or school commitments.

Lockdown was at nine at night, seven days a week. If I had been a card, domino, or chess player, I would have had much to do indoors. There was an excellent, extensive library that was not overcrowded. The yard was available, a place to get fresh air and do weights and other sports. I didn't have an assigned job because I was classified as a student. I could finish high school. I chose to take a vocational course in Refrigeration & Air-Conditioning.

I hadn't been there long when I first walked into the yard. It wasn't Tijuana or the brig, but the boys looked hard. It wasn't going to be easy. A wall of sullen stares and suspicious glances surrounded me as I checked it out. Some of the boys were big. I could judge who was important and who was not by how their peers respected the guys. An impressive-looking guy broke away from a group against the far wall and made a beeline for me. A surge of things went through my head: questions about how I would have to defend myself and how this might play out. I had my hands in my pockets, trying to look casual but fisted, ready to protect myself. I took a few deep breaths. It was elementary and junior high all over again. I'd grown up around but not in gangs. Where was Pi when I needed him in this strange adult life I was leading?

I sensed something familiar.

It was Pi.

"Ese. What the hell did you do?'

I should have guessed. All the home boys were already there. It was like homecoming week at Hollenbeck Junior High. My worries left me when I saw Pi and the others. Pi was a big wheel inside, just as he had been in school. He was in on multiple charges of violent gang activity and attempted murder.

Pi asked, "Did you get framed?"

"Fuck no. I'm guilty as sin."

Pi rubbed my curly hair. "Love you, Bro." I looked around and saw nods and thumbs up from his associates.

* * *

I began the refrigeration and air conditioning service course, took the equivalent of four semesters of typing, and two semesters of general accounting in record time. I handled what I had not done in regular school like a pro at DVI. All I needed to do was read the courses and take a test after each segment. Typing is what I had never gotten right at Hollenbeck. I did at DVI. As I write this, I'm making it sound like I did this in a few weeks. It took time, but I did advance fast.

It reminded me of when I did homework with Patty and how we drove each other. At DVI, I had no one to drive me. Pi and his pals had no interest in learning anything academic or professional.

In County Jail, I had written Luna. I told her that LA cops had arrested me upon my release from the brig.

I still remember one line:

"The messy ink on this letter was caused by my tears that won't stop as long as you are imprisoned."

I wrote Luna from DVI.

I asked Luna for advice on how to get my car from where it was parked when I left El Paso. She wrote back for the address in Los Angeles where I wanted the car taken. Sometime after that, Luna delivered the car to my parents' house. She drove it from El Paso to Los Angeles. It was a long way. Eight hundred miles.

I wrote her. "Luna, you are the kindest person I have ever known. Thank you for taking my car to Los Angeles." I thought of the night she drove me across the border from Mexico to El Paso. "You are the bravest as well."

She wrote back. "Jorjito. I wish you had met me first and married me like you married my sister. We would still be together. I would never have let you leave the Navy." I got chills reading this one.

We exchanged numerous letters over the course of months. It wasn't until I noticed two letters went unanswered that I understood our correspondence had come to an end.

* * *

After completing my daily school lessons, I could pen as many letters as I desired. We were permitted to receive photographs. If anyone wished to visit me, I was granted weekly visits. The visitation guidelines were akin to those in the brig, but the allowed duration was two hours on Saturdays and Sundays. Our correspondence was subject to censorship, but none of my letters were ever returned. We were not allowed to make phone calls. I corresponded with my parents, informing them not to visit. They would send me money monthly for the canteen. Back then, ten dollars could purchase a lot, but it was also significant for them. I couldn't help but feel guilty, as I had always been self-sufficient. I wrote to my mother, instructing her to use the ten dollars they were sending from the proceeds of my car sale. The car was sold swiftly, covering the amount I owed to the bank, with some funds remaining.

* * *

Pi's sentence was like mine. He was committed to the Youth Authority for not more than three years unless the board found him unfit to be released back to society. One of his charges was attempted murder. I never sniveled about it, but the sentencing disparity totally sucked back then, and maybe it still does. My sentence was the same for the theft of thirty-five hundred dollars.

DVI is a city. It's huge. It's possible not to meet up with someone unless you are looking for them. I hadn't seen Mike. One day, I saw him from a distance in the yard. His manslaughter conviction landed him a four-year sentence unless the parole board felt he was not ready to be released to society. Though we'd left County on the same day, Mike's interest in weightlifting and mine in education meant we hadn't crossed paths.

In the yard, I saw Mike was facing a big problem. Crazy, violent, bloody fights happened in the yard all the time. I hadn't been there long, but I'd already seen it happen several times. The yard is bigger than several football fields, and that day, it was the same as always: hard man-boys in orange clustered in groups, some with shirts, some not, basketball goals, concrete, tall wire fencing with gun towers. Ten Mexicans were closing in on Mike. Not belonging to a brotherhood-a gang-made an inmate an outcast, vulnerable to assaults, rapes, extortion, and any unpleasantness you can imagine.

I walked over. I scanned the faces for one I might know. One looked slightly familiar. I thought I recognized the teeth, bad hair, bad attitude, bad tattoos, but I wasn't sure. I might have met him in the yard the first day I'd arrived.

I saw Mike needed help.

"What's happening?" I asked.

The bad tattoo faced me. The others stopped their approach. He broke into a craggy grin that reminded me of Potato Mountain, an hour and a half away from LA.

"Hey. What's up, ese?"

He was a mean-looking motherfucker. His grin was scary. I grinned back. Probably not as frightening.

"Hey, ese, this guy is a friend of mine. You got a problem with him?"

One of the other guys started toward me.

"Yeah, we got a problem with him," one of them said, but it wasn't my Mexican bad teeth buddy.

The friend spat on the ground, then gestured for everyone to stop.

"This dude is tight with Pi," he said. "Cool it."

The silence dragged on. No one moved. The tension in the air was like we were all dropped in the lion's cage at the zoo, except that we were the lions, all on the verge of exploding at the turn of a hair. But we didn't explode. We just stared at each other. After a few minutes, we all fisted, one at a time.

In the center of all this, Mike stood still, his hands clenched, looking like a wrestler ready to explode. He nodded at me once as a greeting, but he was scanning the group, prepared for anything.

"Put your shirt on," I said to him. "It's over."

The Mexican leader put his belt back on. He spoke in Spanish.

"Hey, ese, tell your gabacho friend to learn some manners. When he walks in front of someone, he should excuse himself."

"I think he gets the message," I said in English.

The tension dispersed, and they walked away. Mike and I were left alone.

"I owe you one, George," Mike said, extending his hand.

"Don't sweat it. Come on, let's walk the yard. I'd better introduce you to a friend of mine."

I played it just as I did as a youngster in grammar school. I made friends with those I didn't know through the friends I already had. Pi made that easy for me. I took every opportunity to introduce Mike around, and as far as I know, he never had a problem again. Mike and I became good friends. He enrolled in the refrigeration & air-conditioning class I was in. He always had a grin, and once he kicked the anger, he joked around a lot. He was lucky or clever or probably both. He did very well on any test we had to take. I had to work a lot harder than he did to do as well.

Thanks to my friendship with Pi and his followers, I never had to worry about factions, gang members, or other inmates. I'm not a doormat for anyone and never have been, but I prefer peace and tranquility to fighting. Fighting like I had done at the beginning of boot camp would cost a person more time to do at DVI. I wanted the fuck out as soon as possible and learned when to keep my head down and mind my own business.

My friendship with Pi allowed me to do my own time and leave others to do theirs. When something came down, I walked away. I remembered only that I had seen nothing.

George Hatcher

*　*　*

The violent guys I knew had a soft spot when it came to someone they liked. Tough as they were, they didn't consider it a weakness to cry. We were all emotional when I got out.

"I'll miss you," Pi said as he hugged me.

"I'll miss you, too. Try and behave, Joe."

"Name is Pi."

He sniffed and ran a finger under his nose.

I hugged him again, hugged Mike, and shook hands with the others. I would miss them all. Behind fences and stark concrete, trapped together in savage conditions, these people had been my family.

"I left all the stuff in my room. Go for it," I said, clearing my throat. I had not left everything, though. I kept the bible I'd used as a diary in the brig.

I didn't turn to look back. The sound of well-wishes followed me as far as they could go.

"Better fuck at least five broads for me," Pi yelled.

"And twenty for me."

"And get a blow job for me."

I raised my hand as I walked toward the gate. I felt the tears in my throat and the burning in my eyes, but I didn't cry. I wouldn't cry.

Pi and his followers waited near the front gate to see me off. When I got out, Pi still had two more years before his sentence ended. The parole board cut me loose, but I still did some serious time for three thousand five hundred dollars.

The first gate opened quickly and then closed behind me. A guard took my ID card and checked a photo of me from a file to ensure I was me. I concentrated on the things around me instead of what I felt inside. I heard the metallic click of the solenoid on the second gate. I pushed and walked out.

To freedom.

I was free from prison walls at last. My tears flowed. Twenty-one months had passed since my return from Mexico, most of them spent inside behind bars, behind walls patrolled by guards and gun towers.

The Navy Brig.

County Jail.

DVI.

At last, I was free of the consequences of my mistakes. Or so I believed.

Chapter 26
New Chances, Old Patter

The Youth Authority gave me essential clothing, a bus ticket from Tracy, California, to Los Angeles, and thirty dollars. Despite my financial situation, my spirits were high due to my newfound freedom. The first thing I did was call my family from the nearest payphone. Their voices were a beacon of joy in my day. After the call, I purchased a newspaper and waited for my bus at the station, perusing the classified ads while leaving the rest of the paper behind.

I didn't leave the Youth Authority empty-handed. Apart from the clothes, I had a high school diploma and a certificate of achievement in refrigeration and air-conditioning, both of which I had worked tirelessly to earn. Thanks to Mike, I was also mentally and physically stronger. He had helped me with my studies and introduced me to light weightlifting, which I enjoyed.

When the bus arrived, I found myself amidst a diverse crowd. I felt conspicuous as if my time in prison was visibly etched on me. However, my reflection showed the same person the Navy had recruited. Internally, though, I felt transformed. During the long bus ride, I found myself lost in thoughts of the future and memories of the past. Selena was constantly in my mind despite my attempts to forget her. Luna's last letter had mentioned Selena giving birth to a boy named Armando. I found it easier to distance myself by convincing myself that Sergio, not me, was the father.

During my time in DVI, my nights were often filled with memories of Selena, the happiness we shared, and the life we had built. I tried to shift my thoughts to Luna, with whom I had sporadic communication. Luna was a link to Selena, whom I had moved on from. I often wondered what Patty knew about Thelma's decision to press charges against me. Zoe was frequently on my mind. Probably because she was the last woman I was intimate with before my imprisonment. Christine, my mentor in matters of intimacy, also occupied my thoughts. I was on fire for sure.

I believed there was a significant reason for my time in prison: lessons learned from long nights behind high walls that constantly reminded me of my lost freedoms. Nothing taught loneliness more than mail-less mail calls. At nineteen, with more life experience than most boys my age, I had my whole life ahead. I knew I was a survivor who could handle whatever life threw at me. I was confident I could quickly settle down and find a job, as long as it was legal.

It was a Saturday when I arrived in Los Angeles. My family met me at the bus terminal. Seeing my sister Mary, still a little girl full of life and smiles, gave me a new perspective. I realized how fortunate I was to have a family who cared.

During the drive home, no one mentioned Selena or Juarez. I assumed they respected my silence on the matter. My parents never fully understood that I was sentenced to DVI because Patty's mom had filed charges against me. They thought my imprisonment was due to my desertion from the Navy. I never told my mom that Patty's mom, not my boss at the Pharmacy, had loaned me the money for my brother's lawyer. She would have been devastated if she knew that Patty's mom had filed charges because of that money.

Upon reaching home, I was instantly reminded of Patty, who used to live here. The thought of her mother, Thelma, was the last thing I wanted to entertain. My old bedroom felt vast, a stark contrast to the confined cell I had been living in. The room was a time capsule, preserving the intimate moments Patty and I had shared when this was her mother's house. This was the very room where I had my first sexual encounter. It had been a while since I had been with Patty or anyone. At nineteen, freshly released from prison, my sexual desires were at their peak.

Before retiring for the night, my mother revealed that Patty had tried to reach me during my absence. "How many times did she call?" I asked. "I don't remember," Mom replied, "More than twice." I reassured her. "Mom, Patty is my friend." When Selena had called, my mother had kept my enlistment in the Navy a secret. I wondered what she had told Patty.

"She left her phone number. Let me find it," Mom offered. It was logical for Patty to call here. She had always dialed my parents' number, which had remained unchanged for as long as I could recall.

I dialed Patty's number at six in the evening before settling in. I was eager to hear her voice and didn't pause to think about what I would say if Patty's younger brother or Thelma answered. As the phone rang, I realized my impulsiveness, but it was too late. Patty had already picked up.

"Hey, you called me, but I don't know when it was. I just got home today," I said. "Is this you?" she asked. Hearing Patty's voice brought a rush of memories. Her voice was unmistakable. "You mean you can't tell it's me?" I teased.

She broke down crying. "Hey, if you're upset because I'm calling, I'll hang up," I assured her. "No tears allowed. For me, this is Freedom Day. I've been locked up for twenty-one months. I'm free now."

I found myself wondering how Patty had changed over the past two years. Her hair had always been thick, perfectly in place even when we tumbled in bed. Patty was naturally beautiful and always looked younger than her age. I imagined she might have changed her hairstyle from the short page boy cut with bangs.

"I'm sorry for what my mom did to you. I didn't know until you went in front of the judge. I'm so sorry, George. My mom thought they would force you to pay the money, but she didn't think for a moment they would put you in prison," she confessed.

I partially believed her. I was convinced that Thelma had reported me to the police out of anger when I married someone else and fled to Mexico. "It's done," I told Patty. "I had it coming. When I make it, and I will make it, I will pay your mother. Tell her that."

"Don't be mad at me. I had nothing to do with it," Patty pleaded through tears. I believed in her sincerity. "I'm not mad at you. I'm not mad at your mom, either. It's behind me now."

"I'm your friend, George," she said. "I'm your friend, too," I replied.

* * *

The next day, I dropped my mom and dad off at work. My first stop was the DMV in Montebello. I handed my expired license to the clerk. She was an older woman with thick-rimmed glasses, maybe someone's grandmother.

"I need to renew this," I said.

"Why did you let it expire?" she asked crisply, filling out a form.

"I just did twenty-one months in prison," I heard myself say. That was my total time: four months in the brig, four months in the county jail, and almost fourteen months at DVI.

The lady looked up from the form she was filling in. Her expression softened as she looked at me for what seemed to be a long time. She smiled. She handed me a form.

"Fill this out, bring it back with eight dollars, and I'll renew you with no test."

She smiled—a motherly smile.

"Really?"

"Yes," she said. "You're so honest, you deserve a break."

I left the DMV with a temporary license. I was a happy camper. Sure, I knew how to drive, but tests can be tricky. I considered it a good thing not to have to take it.

About the Author

George Hatcher, formerly a consultant for high-profile wrongful death cases and a successful entrepreneur, has transitioned away from those roles to focus wholeheartedly on his writing. While he no longer consults for lawyers or oversees businesses, George is deeply committed to his literary craft. The COVID-19 pandemic has limited his extensive travels, prompting him to channel his energies into his writing. He now finds solace in Rancho Mirage, California, where he enjoys the company of his wife, Molly, three cats, and two macaws, all while passionately pursuing his latest writing projects.

A longer bio is on his website at http://georgehatcher.com/bio/bio.html